The Woman IN THE Wilderness

A 40-DAY DEVOTIONAL JOURNEY

JOANNA ALONZO

Mahal Kita, Pilipinas.

Contents

A.F.T.L.

to those beloved,
relentlessly pursuing God

"To have found God and still to pursue Him is
the soul's paradox of love." - A.W. Tozer

acknowledgments

Thanks to my mother, Rose, as well as Anna
and Doris for the continuous encouragement
throughout and after the writing and
publishing of this book.

Thanks to Jesus Christ, the Lover of my soul,
my Savior. I am Your beloved, and You are
mine. You and me. Walk on.

introduction

YOUR JOURNEY

You've encountered Him. You remember where, how, and when. The Truth lives inside you, and you know He is real. Maybe your acquaintance with the Almighty is new or perhaps you've known Him your entire life. Either way, you find in your innermost being a deep dissatisfaction. It is caused by a reality acknowledged by everyone who has experienced a real, life-changing encounter with Him:

Once you experience Him, you'll want to experience Him more.

For Him, you would surrender everything. To pursue Him has become your ultimate passion, your divine obsession. To go deeper in your relationship with Him, you are willing to submit yourself to His Lordship. The thought of Him coming to you and saying, "Follow Me" makes your heart leap with delight — even if following Him means embarking on a road of sacrifice. The idea of pursuing Him, dying to self, and embracing the cross makes you tremble inside, but you pursue Him still, because you love Him. You are desperate for Him, so despite the apprehension, you say "Yes". To His bidding, you find your answer will always be "Yes". He is the Priceless Pearl for which you would lay down everything to obtain.

If these are true of you, if these words awaken in you an ache to know Him as He knows you, then the woman in the wilderness is you.

I pray His grace, mercy, and love abound in you as you embark in life's glorious pursuit of He Who is worth giving your life to.

He is alluring you. You sense it, you are familiar with His still, soft whispers, coaxing you to

Come, come as you are,

and you take a step toward His direction, only to find a wilderness in between.

Thus, your journey begins.

Thus, your journey begins.

THE WILDERNESS IN BETWEEN

*S*he stood on top of a hill. Her eyes traveled the distance ahead and set a firm gaze on her destination: the kingdom of glorious light. The One she loved dwelt there, and she had embarked on this journey for Him.

One disconcerting thought occupied her mind: the paradox of having to pursue and seek Someone Who never once left her. She shut her eyes and sensed His abiding presence. He surrounded her and lived within her. He remained a presence felt, yet not fully experienced. His presence not manifested lay at the core of her dissatisfaction. She yearned to know Him as He knew her.

To hear You, to see You, to touch You.

Her heart leaped with anticipation at the thought, but as she opened her eyes, His kingdom stayed atop its distant hill, and she stayed atop hers. She shifted her gaze from her magnificent destination to the vast wasteland keeping her from Him. Her mind echoed a mimic of the psalmist's ardent cries:

> *Oh, that I had the wings of a dove! I*
> *would fly and immediately be at rest—I*
> *would flee far away and stay where He is;*

I would hurry to Him, my Rest, far from
the tempest and storm that bring chaos to
my soul.

She stared with silent wonder at the sun rising over the wilderness. It neared its peak. Soon, blazing heat would wear her down. She clutched the strap of the pouch she brought with her. The pouch contained one enveloped letter: a love letter from Him. He had instructed her to take nothing from her past life with her; thus, her current predicament. Not wanting to start defeated by doubt, she cast away her worries. She recalled a careless, but willing and heartfelt, prayer she once had uttered one lovelorn moment: Take me through the fire.

Once again, she shut her eyes and clung to hope not from within her, but one born out of desire to fellowship with her Beloved. A faith coming from her little knowledge of Who He was. Through the wilderness, she must tread. His voice, a faint whisper, allured her to venture into the great unknown.

Therefore, I am now going to allure
her; I will lead her into the wilderness and
speak tenderly to her.

"I want to be with You," she whispered. "But—"

If possible, let this cup pass from me,

she wanted to echo His words, but she dared not utter the half-meant plea. She recognized she couldn't take any shortcuts, except for one: His redeeming blood, her salvation. Only His sacrifice could cleanse her and make her worthy of this undertaking. So, she became a sojourner. Though she trembled, she made up her mind to pay whatever price necessary to be with Love Divine. Thus, with a hopeful, Lovesick heart, she heaved a sigh and took a step forward, the first among many leading to Him: the Lover of her soul.

VERSES FOR MEDITATION

So I said, "Oh, that I had wings like a dove!
I would fly away and be at rest.
Indeed, I would wander far off,
And remain in the wilderness. Selah
I would hasten my escape
From the windy storm and tempest."
Psalm 55:6-8 (NKJV)

Therefore, behold, I will allure her,
Will bring her into the wilderness,
And speak comfort to her.
Hosea 2:14 (NKJV)

AUTHOR'S REFLECTIONS

At certain points in our walk with God, we've been in this place. We've envisioned what our relationship with God could be like and what being part of His kingdom means. Yet, reality is different from what we hope and envision. We struggle to spend time with Him, to obey, and to focus. Thousands of distractions — the windy storm and tempest — pull us away from Him.

We struggle.

And in the midst of the struggle, we hear His constant, alluring voice, coaxing us to come away with Him. We want this. We want His kingdom to come alive in us, to thrive in our daily comings and goings.

Passion becomes a hunger, and discipline becomes a thirst.

None can satisfy but Him.

Consider this an invitation to spend time every

day to come away. Wander far off into the wilderness, and let Him speak to you in the unknown.

He is waiting.

May the Spirit be to you as the wings of a dove that you may soar into His presence and be at rest.

day 2

THE RIDGE & THE DOVE

The sun blazed over the arid desert. How long would she last in the water?

She trudged up a sand hill. Her mind made up an ache in her shoulders caused by the weight of her empty pouch as she plodded upwards. When she reached the top of the small hill, her face fell at the sight presented to her. A sprawling mountain range stood in her way.

How am I to get past this?

She shook her head. The range hadn't existed when she had looked at the horizon, atop the hill where her journey had begun. She clenched her jaw and ground her teeth in frustration. What other surprises would this journey hold? Still, she refused to give up and continued walking.

If no way exists for me to get past the mountains, I should turn back.

Something deep within her screamed against the idea, but if He wouldn't act on her behalf, how else was she supposed to continue?

Her helplessness without Him made her cringe.

She dragged her feet until she arrived at the foot of the mountains an hour or two later. By that time, the lack of water parched her throat and exhausted her. She rested her back against the mountain. Now what? Nothing was here. How could anyone survive this journey?

Despondent, she slanted her form against the rock-solid wall behind her, slid down, and sat on the sand. She shut her eyes as she mulled over her predicament.

If I turn back, to what am I returning? I prefer to die in search for Him than live forever apart from Him. I can't turn back.

In that moment, an odd sight caught her eye. Fluttering wings carried a dove past her. Full of grace. Pure. Its whiteness, which glimmered against the sun's rays, provided a stark contrast to the desert's drab surroundings. She blinked her eyes several times and smiled with relief to find that, though far from her, the dove existed. There was yet life to be found in the wilderness! But, her relief proved temporary, because the dove flew right into the rocky mountain. She gasped, expecting the bird to crash into the cliffs. Instead, it disappeared from view.

She creased her brows in confusion. She ran toward where the dove had disappeared. Upon reaching the spot, a narrow valley in between two giant mountain ranges came within view.

A smile crept over her parched lips. Her beloved had hidden ways in the wilderness.

Manna

VERSES FOR MEDITATION

I'm not saying that I have this all together, that I have it made. But I am well on my way, reaching out for Christ, who has so wondrously reached out for me. Friends, don't get me wrong: By no means do I count myself an expert in all of this, but I've got my eye on the goal, where God is beckoning us onward—to Jesus. I'm off and running, and I'm not turning back.
Philippians 3:12-14 (MSG)

So let's keep focused on that goal, those of us who want everything God has for us. If any of you have something else in mind, something less than total commitment, God will clear your blurred vision—you'll see it yet! Now that we're on the right track, let's stay on it.
Philippians 3:15-16 (MSG)

AUTHOR'S REFLECTIONS

When we make a conscious decision to follow hard after God, odds are we will find obstacles along the way. Like many saints who have gone before us, we don't turn back.

If Jesus is the heart, the soul, the ultimate quest of this journey we've embarked on, then we can't afford to give up. In moments when we find ourselves facing insurmountable odds, we ask ourselves: *Do I want Him? Do I want everything He has for me — His heart, His mind, His smile?*

If we can't answer with a hearty, sincere "Yes," we discover the Holy Spirit willing to help. He changes our focus and becomes our Guide. He enables us to keep our eyes on our destination: Jesus Himself. Despite the circumstances surrounding us, the mountains blocking us, we allow the Holy Spirit to do His work in us. When we do, He is faithful to open our eyes and show us the way to go.

Are you tired and thirsty? Are your circumstances overwhelming you, and you can't see a way out? Don't give up. Stop. Breathe. Rest. Refocus. Let the Holy Spirit show you The Way.

day 3

The Valley, Dark & Deep

Rapturous glee sprung up from her tired soul. And yet, upon closer inspection, apprehension replaced her joy. Her eyes failed to reach the end of the dark, foreboding valley. She shuddered and retreated. But, what other way was there? Clenching her fists, she decided to push through. Still, the familiar voice of doubt shook her resolve, and made her dread the possibility of being trapped in the valley before nightfall.

What will I do then?

As she stood unmoving and struggled to decide her next step, a soft breeze cooled her sun-parched skin. With the breeze, came a soft whisper:

> *Blessed are those whose strength*
> *is in Me, who have set their hearts on*
> *pilgrimage.*

She breathed a deep sigh and closed her eyes to savor the soothing wind and bask in the marvelous light those words brought to the dark, fearful crevices of her soul.

I will go from strength to strength.

With a determination that surprised even her, she gathered her courage and took a step toward the small opening. She had taken only a few strides forward when an unmistakable rippling sound stopped her on her tracks. She couldn't believe her ears! Water?!

She turned around to look at the path she had just passed. On the exact spot where she had taken her first step into the valley, water gushed out of the ground.

She stood rooted to her spot as right before her eyes, a spring formed in the desert. She gawked in disbelief for a few more heartbeats before her thirst overcame her. Bending forward, she scooped water in her hands and drank. The water — unlike any other — refreshed not only her body, but her soul.

A renewed sense of hope arose from her depths.

Why sulk and be so downcast?

A smile formed on her face as she continued her journey, walking deeper and deeper into the unknowns of the wilderness. Doubt and apprehension left her. Convinced He would take care of her throughout her adventure, she brought the spark of expectation in her soul into the recesses of the dark, uncharted valley. Belief grew within her:

finding Him outweighs whatever the cost.

Manna

VERSES FOR MEDITATION

Why, my soul, are you downcast? Why so disturbed within me? Put your hope in God, for I will yet praise him, my Savior and my God.
Psalm 43:5

Blessed are those whose strength is in You, whose hearts are set on pilgrimage. As they pass through the Valley of Baka, they make it a place of springs; the autumn rains also cover it with pools. They go from strength to strength, till each appears before God in Zion.
Psalm 84:5-7

AUTHOR'S REFLECTIONS

We forget too easily. We forget we are not the same people who took that life-changing first step to follow God Almighty. If we compare where we began and where we are now, we have gone from strength to strength.

We fail to remember we've gone past treks through our own "Valleys of Baka" — translated as valleys of weeping. And, our tears became a source of restoration and refreshment, not only to ourselves, but also to others.

We forget, and we despair, and we find our souls downcast, our minds bewildered, but we've decided not to turn back. Through the doubts and apprehensions, we take that step forward in our journey. One foot after another. A day, an hour, a minute, a second at a time.

And we walk on, because we set our hearts on this pilgrimage, and though we sometimes falter, we pick ourselves up, dust ourselves off, and will ourselves to keep going.

It is His strength that enables us to do this. This is where we are strong. A kind leader of mine once told me: *You are strongest when you are weak.* This has rung true with every step I have taken toward him in moments of weakness. He has become my Strength, my Source of refreshment.

This is our story as His church, His bride. We go from strength to strength, even when emotions say otherwise, until we see Him face to face.

Take a moment to reflect today. In what areas of your life — areas of weakness maybe — has He given you grace to go from strength to strength? Are you thankful? Is it something worth celebrating? Is He not deserving of our worship?

Why so downcast, soul? Put your trust in God.

LIGHTNING IN THE DARKNESS

er heart pounded against her chest as panic consumed her. The sun set over the horizon. Darkness threatened to spill over the narrow valley, its end still nowhere in sight. With all the strength she could muster, she sped up her already frenzied pace. Nothing. The valley — long, dark, and winding — trapped her within its walls.

Not until twilight did she surrender to the inevitable. She needed to spend a night in the darkness of that plain. Somewhere at the center of the ever-increasing chaos in her soul, His peace remained. Still, her mind urged her to give in to fear, for she was but human, anxious over what horrors her first night in the wilderness would bring.

She struggled to make her soul return to His peace, to calm in chaos, but the attempt proved futile. When she reached the point where peace seemed impossible, and she resigned herself to fear, she heard what she desired to hear. His inaudible whisper reminded her of truths she had to learn to cling to.

> *Though you walk through the valley of*
> *the shadow of death, fear no evil for I am*
> *with you.*

A tear fell down her cheek as the reality of how much

she needed Him sank in. She uttered, with a heartfelt desperation, one of Asaph's cries:

O God, do not keep silent; be not quiet,
O God, be not still. See how Your enemies
are astir, how Your foes rear their heads.

In answer to her prayer, a thunderous sound filled the heavens and one strike of lightning lit the dark night sky, illuminating glimpses of the shadows plaguing her. The lightning hit the ground with so much force, she jolted and shrieked. Awe, however, replaced her fright, because where the lightning bolt had stricken, a pillar of fire rose from the ground to the open heavens.

The darkness radiated with brilliant light.

Manna

VERSES FOR MEDITATION

Even though I walk
through the darkest valley,
I will fear no evil,
for you are with me;
your rod and your staff,
they comfort me.
Psalm 23:4a

O God, do not remain silent;
do not turn a deaf ear,
do not stand aloof, O God.
See how your enemies growl,
how your foes rear their heads.
Psalm 83:1-2

AUTHOR'S REFLECTIONS

With darkness comes fear of the unknown and fear of the unseen.

Many saints experienced the "dark night of the soul": hopelessness and anguish, which comes with dread of a future that might hold no light. In seasons of a soul's dark night, we question His involvement in our lives. Silent and unyielding, distant and aloof, he has seemingly abandoned us.

We experience these periods, and we despair, but He is present even when we are unaware. He cultivates something deep within us. He instills a sense of discipline and direction — the rod and the staff — and we can find comfort in knowing He is at work, making us holy as He is holy.

These times make us vulnerable to the enemy's taunts, and it's easy to succumb, to believe the lies, to resent what feels like abandonment. Instead, we cry out to Him, because the fact remains: He is God, and He is good, and no matter what happens, we have set our hearts on pilgrimage.

So, through darkness, through valleys, through fire, we keep walking.

Have you encountered the dark night of the soul? What disciplines, guideposts, and deposits of faith have these seasons instilled in you? Find comfort in the progress towards holiness and trust: this too shall pass.

day 5

THE PILLAR OF FIRE

The firelight eradicated the forces of darkness clawing at her. She remembered how Job's young and poor excuse of a friend — misguided as he was — had spoken truth:

He fills His hands with lightning and
commands it to strike its mark.

The fire blocked the path leading deeper into the valley. She stood before it without the slightest inkling what to do. The fire was reassuring and taunting at the same time. While it comforted her that He was present and in control, the pillar of flames also blazed with an inescapable truth:

Be holy for I am holy. Without holiness,
no one will see the Lord.

She shuddered at the choice circling her mind: Go back or get consumed by His fire.

She had already known this was coming, for He had warned her beforehand.

Fire goes before Me and consume my
foes on every side. My lightning lights up

the world; the earth sees and trembles.

To get to Him, I must go through the fire.

She stood her ground, fists clenched, ready for battle. Too terrified to take a step toward the fire, but too determined a sojourner to go back to where she had come from, she stood at an impasse. She gritted her teeth even as she mumbled, "I can't go back."

The standstill seemed to last forever as she stood stubborn and motionless, aware of what she needed to do, but afraid of doing it, so she called for His help.

Give me the courage to go through this.

Unearthly calm swept away her qualms as she surrendered her every apprehension to unwavering trust in Him. She closed her eyes, breathed a sigh, and gathered all the will she had to take one tiny step forward, closer to the blazing fire. Little did she know how powerful a step of obedience could be. The moment her feet touched the ground, the flames surged through her and within a few moments, fire consumed the woman in the wilderness.

Manna

VERSES FOR MEDITATION

*He fills His hands with lightning and commands it to
strike its mark.*
Job 36:32

*Fire goes before Him
And consumes His foes on every side.
His lightning lights up the world;
the earth sees and trembles.*
Psalm 97:3-4

...without holiness no one will see the Lord.
Hebrews 12:14b

AUTHOR'S REFLECTIONS

The fear of the Lord, how often the wise speak of it!

We think of God as Father. We think of Him as Friend, Provider, Comforter. And it's true. He is! But, in the familiarity, as we draw ever closer to Him, we forget He is also Almighty. He is Omnipotent. He is the Great I Am.

When faced with His power, how do our hearts respond? Are we reminded that He is not a God Who exists to fulfill our every demand? Do we find comfort, conviction, or contempt in our hearts when faced with the Greatness of a Holy God?

The wilderness is a place where we empty ourselves to encounter Who He is, not Who we want Him to be. The wilderness is not a place of convenience, but a place where we meet Him in the fire and the fury. He tests us and refines us in the fire of that testing.

He asks for our surrender and asks for our "yes".

Whatever you are going through right now, when you look at what's ahead, if you had little hope and great dread about the trials to come, would you still surrender? Will you give Him your "yes"?

day 6

THE MORNING

Dawn brushed over the quiet valley and revealed her motionless form as she awakened from a deep sleep. She opened her tear-stained eyes.

Did I dream it all up? Did I only imagine the wilderness, the spring, and the fire?

She scanned her surroundings with one swift gaze and realized it was all real. In the wilderness, she had found — or lost — her way into a narrow valley and its swelling springs, pitch black nights, and lightning fire.

She paused and gasped as complete remembrance of the night before caught up with her: she had walked through a fire that had consumed her.

She had expected a change after walking through the flames. Though she didn't know what transformation she had hoped to happen, she hadn't expected to find herself the same way she had been the night before. In truth, she felt more broken and alone than she had the day before.

She clung to words, which He had once spoken to her, a faint memory of Him and His Love.

*It's what you trust in, but don't yet see
that will keep you going.*

She fought to keep her faith and hope steady and reminded herself He yet awaited her; the journey will take her to Him. Conflict raged within her, for in all honesty, hopelessness and loneliness suffocated her senses. She cried out for a visible, tangible hope in which she could be confident, yet all she could hold on to were recollections of His promises. Tears flowed down her face as fragments of her desire to view the unseen, listen to the unheard, and caress the intangible revisited her.

How can I trust Your word? Your promises are all I have to cling to.

Her thoughts mimicked the heart of the 119th psalm repeatedly.

I've only begun this journey and already, I'm weighed down by my weakness, my transgressions. They pull me down like burdens I can't carry. Why didn't the flames consume these?

Her disillusionment increased as she continued to ponder on her woes. She closed her eyes as the scorching sun, rising to its peak, burned against her skin. She sensed the familiar ache within, the one caused by her yearning for Him.

Where are You, my Love?

No answer. Today, when she needed His assurance most, He chose to be silent, save for His words engraved deep within her heart.

Return to your rest, my soul, for the Lord has been good to you.

She recalled the refreshing water from the springs and how it revived her weary soul. Didn't His lightning light up the dark night and dispel the shadows that threatened to devour her? Had she forgotten how He had allured her, how vagrant breezes had carried His whispers to her?

> *The earth is filled with Your love, O Lord. Teach me Your ways. Save me for I am Yours. Your word is a lamp to my feet and a light for my path. Sustain me according to Your promise... do not let my hopes be dashed.*

Clinging to His word and the renewed faith that came with it, she slew her disillusion. She couldn't give in to discouragement, so with heartfelt candor, she yelled out, "Praise my Lord!"

As she hoped it would, inexplicable joy surged within her and filled her with the kind of spirit she needed to press on in her journey.

Manna

VERSES FOR MEDITATION

It's what we trust in but don't yet see that keeps us going.
2 Corinthians 5:7 (MSG)

Return to your rest, my soul, for the Lord has been good to you.
Psalm 116:7

The earth is filled with your love, Lord;
teach me your decrees.
...
I gain understanding from your precepts;
therefore I hate every wrong path.
Your word is a lamp for my feet,
a light on my path.
...
Sustain me, my God, according to your promise, and I will live; do not let my hopes be dashed.
Psalm 119:64,104-105,116

AUTHOR'S REFLECTIONS

Most likely, we've experienced fiery encounters with God, precious moments when we come face-to-face with His astounding glory. Maybe we went to a church camp or a conference. Or we worshiped Him in the quietness and intimacy of our bedrooms. We then went back to the routine of our daily lives — the grind, the messes, the challenges, the struggles. We fell into old patterns and comfort zones, and we forgot our divine encounters. Almost like they never happened.

Peter walked on water when he set his eyes on Christ and sank on water once he set his eyes on the waves and the storm. Can you relate?

We trust and hope and grasp at faith, but life keeps kicking. And we lose sight of the hope we're clinging to.

But the earth is filled with His love! If only we open faith's eyes, we will meet His goodness and His faithfulness.

Remember those moments of encounter. While in the wilderness, when tempted to murmur as the Israelites did, remember the Red Sea moments, when He came through and parted the seas for us. Don't forget His greatness and power. Don't forget His love.

And as you remember, give Him the praise due His Name. But, even when you struggle to remember, praise Him anyway.

day 7

THE SLITHER

She smiled as she skipped through a valley winding toward what looked like infinity. The valley got narrower and narrower as she went on, but she didn't notice. The sun, furious in its blaze, did little to faze her. Her dwindling water supply, though not as refreshing as the day before, failed to instill a single seed of worry in her.

Her peace, her reason to rejoice, relied on the confidence that He would watch over her. She held a level of pride at the peace and happiness she experienced and gave herself subconscious congratulations to acknowledge her progress. The misguided glee caused her blindsided shock when, after turning a corner along the valley's winding pathway, she encountered something she hadn't prepared to find.

Numb at first as she stood still, she took in the sight. The shock wore off, replaced by a stirring in her stomach and a multitude of thoughts running across her mind all at once.

"No, no, no..." she whispered. She clenched and unclenched her fists in utter disbelief. "This doesn't make any sense."

Right before her, the two ranges, which formed the valley, closed. She reached the end of the valley and met a dead end.

All joy, all peace, all thoughts of good things and hope unseen melted away as disappointment sank in. "All for nothing," she whispered.

A voice came. Strange, but familiar.

> Did He really tell you to embark on this journey?

Yes, of course He– She paused. *Did He?* Doubt consumed her.

> In vain. My journey proved in vain.

The voice reinforced her doubts.

> A passage in His Word says, "What is man that He would care for him, the son of man that He would think of him?" Why would He want you?

She remembered that passage.

> I am but a breath, my days are like a fleeting shadow. Who do I think I am? Why would He, in His glorious perfection, want me? I'm a fool to go on this journey.

The hint of mockery was unmistakable as the voice delivered its final blow.

> Turn back. Life is short. It's not too late for you to live your life as you please while you still can.

She creased her brows as her spirit — recognizing something amiss — cried out within her. The voice, belonging to someone who had once been her close counselor — sweet and alluring — had plagued her many times in the past.

Now, to her, it sounded like nothing but an enticing hiss, a reminder of a familiar slither, a winding away from Truth.

She cast aside the doubt, the shame, the self-condemning magnification of her obvious weaknesses and imperfections and tried to recall the Love of her life.

His word returned to her:

His love endures forever.

Another still, small, calming voice brought her the peace she needed.

Though the LORD is on high, He looks
upon the lowly.

She stared at the dead end, and though she didn't understand, she trusted He would grant her a way through.

Manna

VERSES FOR MEDITATION

*what is mankind that you are mindful of them,
human beings that you care for them?*
Psalm 8:4

...His love endures forever.
Psalm 136

*Though the Lord is exalted, he looks kindly on the
lowly; though lofty, he sees them from afar.*
Psalm 138:6

AUTHOR'S REFLECTIONS

When we encounter His power and glory, we see Him for all He is — His greatness, His wonder, His magnificence — and the enemy can use that knowledge against us. He uses God's Word against us, the same way he did to Jesus in the wilderness, to cast doubt about God's love for us.

In these occasions, we can't focus on our own weakness or sinfulness. We can't even dwell on the circumstances that surround us. Instead, we return to His Word and remember His promises. We remember Who He says He is, and we hold on to that.

Do you believe God is Who He says He is? Do you believe that even in His greatness, He wants us, He chose us, enough to give His life for us? He is not some prideful, tyrannical monarch who sits on high, caring little for His lowly subjects. In all His glory, Jesus chose to become a man, so He knows what it is like to be us. Because He understands, He doesn't look at us with disgust or condemnation.

May the truth sink deep into our hearts: He desires us and longs for our fellowship. He doesn't want us to give up.

So, no matter how the enemy throws lies our way, no matter how impossible our circumstances are, we can't give up. He said He will make a way. Trust that He will.

day 8

THE GLASS WALL

His love endures forever, His song echoes.
Even in His glory and perfection, does He
not understand me? He created my inmost
being. Has He not placed His eyes on me?

She faced the dead end once again. Her heart drummed a hard, steady rhythm within her. She sank to her knees, shut her eyes, and cried out to Him. "Do You not perceive the intentions of my heart? Did You not search my motives? Do You not understand my mind? How I fear You in Your holiness, purity, righteousness, and splendor! The one thing driving me in this journey, my only source of hope, is Your sweet, wondrous, unfailing love. Listen to my cry, even to the contents of my heart, which my words fail to express."

She frowned when she heard the slithering voice respond to her cries.

You are a fool. This journey will take you
nowhere. You waste your time.

Despite the hisses, His promise sank in to her wanting heart and restless soul: The LORD delights in those Who fear Him, who put their hope in His unfailing love.

A supernatural calm enveloped her when she recognized the spite in the hissing slither. In its cowardice, the tempter slunk away at her heart's mention of His Word.

She opened her eyes and hoped to find Him with her. But, only the dead end greeted her vision, so she shut her eyes again and whispered a silent plea:

> *Answer me quickly, LORD; my spirit fails. Do not hide Your face from me or I will be like those who go down to the pit. Let the morning bring me word of Your unfailing love for I have put my trust in You. Show me the way I should go, for to You I entrust my life.*

Before she could finish saying the words, the earth shook. Her eyes shot open. Astonished by the sight that presented itself before her, the final verse in the final psalm revisited her memories.

> *Let everything that has breath praise the LORD. Praise the LORD.*

Her mouth agape and her eyes wide open, she knelt on the ground and absorbed the astonishing sight before her. The two ranges parted to reveal an opening, and she fell short of breath at the sight of the wonder ahead of her. The wilderness revealed a garden full of wondrous flora and fauna. With colorful, brilliant, and luminescent wings, a moth flew by her and landed on a glowing stargazer of the shade of sapphires speckled with silver.

Her heart drummed an accelerated, erratic beat as she stood up, eager to experience the wonders of the garden, so she ran to it only to find herself shocked. As she was about to step into the garden, she hit a glass wall.

Manna

VERSES FOR MEDITATION

Search me, God, and know my heart;
test me and know my anxious thoughts.
See if there is any offensive way in me,
and lead me in the way everlasting.
Psalm 139:23-24

the Lord delights in those who fear Him,
who put their hope in His unfailing love.
Psalm 147:11

Answer me quickly, Lord;
my spirit fails.
Do not hide your face from me
or I will be like those who go down to the pit.
Let the morning bring me word of your unfailing love,
for I have put my trust in you.
Show me the way I should go,
for to you I entrust my life.
Psalm 143:7-8

Let everything that has breath praise the Lord.
Praise the Lord.
Psalm 150:6

AUTHOR'S REFLECTIONS

Has there been a point in your life where you kept the faith, trusted in God, and held on to His promises, yet you still hit one wall after another? You get past one dead end only to see another one before you?

Sometimes, in our Christian walk, we seem to go from test to trial to challenge in a never-ending obstacle course of faith. Daunted and exhausted, we entertain the notion of giving up, because it doesn't seem like we're making any progress. Though it may seem that way sometimes, if we step back and make a fair assessment of the situation, we've also been going from one encounter to another. He has strengthened our hearts and toughened us up. We may not be aware, but we change in the process.

Given this revelation, our heart's response becomes more of praise rather than complaint, trust rather than doubt. In this, He delights.

If we look back to when we first started the journey, we recognize that from the beginning, we were aware the journey would be difficult, but we were still excited. Now, the excitement has faded. We felt better when we started than we do facing yet another hurdle, but we've gone this far in our walk with the Lord, and He has been faithful.

We already experienced a lot of obstacles, and there'll be more along the way. What's our hearts' response? Is it of murmuring or of praise? For as long as we have breath, He will deserve our praise. No matter what our circumstances are, we can still praise Him.

day 9

THE SECRET DOOR

H er face contorted as she stared at the glass wall before her.

What's going on? This dead end, a cruel taunt, shows me something I long for, then takes it from me when I want it the most.

A chill traveled from the soles of her feet to the nape of her neck when she heard an audible hiss.

<u>Did you really think it would be easy?</u>

She furrowed her brows and mused over her predicament. Right before her anxiety got the best of her, a smile lit up her face, and her eyes brightened with delight.

Yes, I do! Why can't the next step of my journey be easy? He rewards faith, no matter how weak, does He not?

His assurances flooded her mind:

"Blessed are they who hunger and thirst for righteousness for they will be filled."

"Come to Me, all you who are weary and burdened, and I will give you rest. Take My yoke upon you and learn from Me, for I am gentle and humble in heart, and you will find rest for your souls. For My yoke is easy and my burden is light."

"Ask and it will be given to you; seek and you will find; knock and the door will be opened to you. For everyone who asks receives; the one who seeks finds; and to the one who knocks, the door will be opened."

Yearning overpowered her fears as her eyes flickered with a hope not her own.

All I ask is to be with Him not riches, not fame, not anything else other than to know Him as He knows me. Why would He deny me that?

She turned her head toward the slithering voice. The sly creature taunting her was nowhere in sight, but she sensed its presence, and she recognized: in this battle of wills, she had come out the victor. She remembered the words her Beloved once spoke to her and held on to her faith in Him, despite how much the fulfillment of His promises seemed out of reach.

Sudden understanding took over her mind and soul as she examined the glass wall.

Some things aren't as they seem. What if the glass wall is a door?

She mustered all the faith given her by He Who is Faithful and knocked on the glass.

True to His Word, the glass door opened.

Manna

VERSES FOR MEDITATION

Blessed are those who hunger and thirst for righteousness, for they will be filled.
Matthew 5:6

"Come to me, all you who are weary and burdened, and I will give you rest. Take my yoke upon you and learn from me, for I am gentle and humble in heart, and you will find rest for your souls. For my yoke is easy and my burden is light."
Matthew 11:28-30

Ask and it will be given to you; seek and you will find; knock and the door will be opened to you. For everyone who asks receives; the one who seeks finds; and to the one who knocks, the door will be opened.
Matthew 7:7-8

AUTHOR'S REFLECTIONS

I can't count the number of times I've felt like He's showing something I want, only to discover it's something I can't have. At least not yet. The object, ambition, or desire, which seems so within reach, eludes me.

Have you been through what I'm saying?

When experiencing this, I try to remember He is not a cruel God, prone to taunt us and lead us on for no purpose. All His ways are intentional and hold love at its core.

What is the proper response when life snatches away what we desire? Do we blame Him? Or do we treat these moments as opportunities to assess what we are pursuing in our journey? Is it Him? Or is it what we stand to gain should we find Him? Can we, with boldness, say we're after God? Not fame, nor wealth, nor anything other than the Lover of Souls?

The trials in our lives are signposts pointing us to Him. They are our detours from the path we assume we want to the path He planned for us—the way we prayed for when we desired to obey His will.

These are times when we set our minds, emotions, and eyes on Him. If we ask, seek, and knock for Him, then why wouldn't He open the door leading to Him? So what are you waiting for? Knock.

day 10

THE SYCAMORE

Awed and expectant, she entered the garden. She had walked only a few steps in when a loud, booming voice, with a cheerful tone, broke her reverie.

"Well, hello there!"

She scanned her surroundings to discoveer whom the voice came from, but she was alone. She gulped and muttered, "Hello?"

"I'm right here, young one."

To her side, a towering sycamore tree, with a face of bark carved into its trunk, smiled at her. Her mouth dropped open. She considered running as far away as possible, but the sycamore beamed such a hearty smile at her, it seemed rude not to smile back.

She tilted her head to the side and inspected the tree. How was it speaking to her?

"You've been crying, child."

"How do you know?" she asked.

"The wind carries whispers from all corners of this wilderness. For example, it has come to my knowledge that you, child, are starving." One of the sycamore's branches handed her an apple while the other pointed to a nearby brook. "Get a drink. Have a bite. Sit down and listen for you are not in this forest by accident, and I am tasked to give you counsel."

A forest. Not a garden. She frowned, glanced at the sycamore, and for a couple of seconds, stared at the apple in her hand. Too mystified to move from her spot, her gaze drifted back to the sycamore, then to the brook, then back to the sycamore.

"Well, move along, child! You don't have roots like I do! Now's not the time to settle."

As she walked to the brook to fill her container with water, she scratched her head with one hand and took a bite from the apple with the other.

The sycamore rambled as she went about her task. "So you've set out to seek the Lover of souls, heh? A treasure worth seeking, I say! Nay! The only treasure worth seeking. Definitely!"

She closed her container and sat on the ground in front of the tree.

How does the tree know my journey's purpose? How could a tree know anything?

Before she could voice out her questions, the tree began talking again.

"Sometimes we find ourselves too weak, too powerless to find Him. We struggle with our weaknesses and make too many excuses for ourselves. Live by what the Good Book says!" As the tree spoke, its branches swung in the air with every point and emphasis he made. However, it stopped moving and a solemn expression replaced its glee when it recited,

"Words kill, words give life; they're either poison or fruit – you choose.'

'What have our words been feeding our souls? Words spoken out are words we declare to others. Words believed are words we declare to ourselves. What have our thoughts been saying, child? The Good Book says,'

'For as he thinks in his heart, so is he'.

'If what we think in our hearts defines us—" two of its longest branches flew in the air "—what are we then?!"

Well, you are a tree. The fact that you're talking at all baffles me. What are you indeed?

She opened her mouth to voice out her response, but the sycamore's sigh told her it wasn't done talking, so she ate her apple, drank water, and listened.

The tree still had more to say.

Manna

VERSES FOR MEDITATION

Words kill, words give life;
they're either poison or fruit—you choose.
Proverbs 18:21 (MSG)

For as he thinks in his heart, so is he.
Proverbs 23:7a (NKJV)

AUTHOR'S REFLECTIONS

We ponder on two points here: the value of counsel from those wiser and more rooted than us and the power of our thoughts to either make or break us.

The wilderness may be wide, stark, and barren, but we don't need to go through it alone. Many have gone before us, and they stand as signposts for our journey. It benefits us to take some time to stop and listen to the wisdom, knowledge, and understanding they offer.

Next, we consider our words, because the words we think and the words we say hold power. Examine what goes on in your mind. Do they build you up or tear you down? If your thoughts destroy you, perhaps it's time to seek out encouragement, counsel, and a reason to rejoice from those willing to share their wisdom with you.

*Note: A conversation with my uncle inspired the sycamore tree. We attended a prayer night watch, and for reasons I won't go into, the other intercessors asked him and me to step out of the prayer room. (We didn't do anything bad, I promise.) My uncle, an elder in our church, took the opportunity to share what he's been learning to me. He shared with such joy and exuberance.

Thus, the day after, The Sycamore Tree became part of this wilderness journey.

day 11

THE BENEFACTOR

"The Good Book says the renewing of our minds transforms us and is necessary for us to know His perfect will.'

'Do you remember when Abraham cast out Hagar into the wilderness, and she reached a desperate point, waiting for her beloved Ishmael to die? The angel of the Lord appeared and suddenly, she saw a well! I have a theory that the well had always been there. Blinded by her situation, she didn't perceive its presence, and only when the good Lord gave her hope did she receive the ability to see. Don't you think it's a good theory?"

She nodded and said, "It's interesting for sure."

"Our mindset is the problem, understand? Our circumstances consume us so much, we forget about His benefits, and we can't enjoy something we've forgotten, can we? Such a sad thing when we fail to remember His benefits, especially when they're listed so clearly in one of the psalms. They come in tandems.'

'He forgives your iniquities and heals all your diseases. He redeems your life from destruction and crowns you with loving-kindness and tender mercies. He satisfies your mouth with good things and renews your youth like the eagle's.'

'Isn't that wonderful?!"

The tree's branches moved all over the place, its leaves flying around like confetti, celebrating the truths it spouted out. The tree's joy lightening her heart, she chuckled as she nodded and said, "Thank you for reminding me of how wonderful He is."

"You have to understand though: you must claim your benefits, because they are not automatic. You have to remember them, so you can claim them when you need them." The tree paused for a few seconds before its eyes sparkled with delight. "Oh, oh! Do you know what it means for God to renew your youth like the eagle's?"

She shook her head, but she was certain she was about to find out.

VERSES FOR MEDITATION

Do not conform to the pattern of this world, but be transformed by the renewing of your mind. Then you will be able to test and approve what God's will is—his good, pleasing and perfect will.
Romans 12:2

*Praise the Lord, my soul,
and forget not all his benefits —
who forgives all your sins
and heals all your diseases,
who redeems your life from the pit
and crowns you with love and compassion,
who satisfies your desires with good things
so that your youth is renewed like the eagle's.*
Psalm 103:2-5

AUTHOR'S REFLECTIONS

The battle is in our minds. We hear those words so often, they become a cliche. Though they sometimes lose depth or meaning, they are no less true.

Our mind sometimes tricks us into holding as truth a perception that may be a lie. Whatever thoughts are going through your mind, remember the benefits of being a child of God, and believe:

- He has forgiven all your sins
- He has healed all your diseases
- He has redeemed your life from the pit
- He has crowned you with love and compassion
- He has satisfied your desires with good things
- He has renewed your youth like the eagle's

Let your mind dwell on that while you praise Him.

49

THE MOLTING EAGLE

"**W**e recognize a kingdom pattern here. To go from strength to strength, from glory to glory has something to do with the molting process of the eagle. There comes a point when an eagle molts, its feathers fall out, it weakens, its claws lose its sharpness. The eagle is so helpless, even the smallest snake can kill it. What the eagle does is it perches itself in a place where it can have the sun shine on it. Other eagles, who have already survived this process, feed the eagle, because they know what it is going through. Some eagles survive this process and others do not, but those that do, come out stronger. Their youth is renewed, but better, stronger, and wiser. That is what it means for our youth to be renewed like the eagle's. Don't you think that's amazing?"

Again, she nodded in response as she took another bite from the apple and brushed away some of the tree's leaves that fell on her lap.

"We must remember, child." The sycamore took on a more solemn tone, but the glint of glee never left its eyes. "Remember what our quest is. We need to be transformed by the renewing of our minds. But to be transformed to what? We are to be transformed into His likeness. Remember Adam and Eve, who were made in His image before they were given authority and dominion over the earth. Always remember: He is Love. Who are you? Are you Love?"

At this, she couldn't bring herself to nod. Was she Love?

"Your quest is to be like Him."

The sycamore stopped for dramatic effect, before it heaved a sigh. As if running out of time, it gently prodded her up with its branches.

"Now, child, that's all I have time to say. Move on now before the sun sets. His Word will Light your path when it gets dark, so do not worry if you are caught in this forest at night. Journey on now, and believe He will keep you safe, but remember: go from strength to strength. Do not dwell on your weaknesses. Set your eyes on Him, so you may be like Him. I, on the other hand, must go now."

You're a tree. Where could you possibly be going?

She was about to ask, but whatever was talking to her had disappeared. The tree was once again just a tree. She hoped to meet him again as she remembered a line derived from a psalm she'd been keeping in her heart:

We will go from strength to strength
until we see You face to face.

Strength to strength. More like Him. She smiled.

Thank You, Lord, for the sycamore.

51

Manna

Verses for Meditation

Blessed and greatly favored is the man whose strength is in You, In whose heart are the highways to Zion. Passing through the Valley of Weeping (Baca), they make it a place of springs; The early rain also covers it with blessings. They go from strength to strength [increasing in victorious power]; Each of them appears before God in Zion.
Psalm 84:5-7 (AMP)

Author's Reflections

God meant for us to live victorious lives. When eagles molt, they are often misunderstood by those who haven't been where they are. It's those who've gone through the molting process who understand how weak the molting eagle is, and how strong the eagle will be, should it survive.

Our seasons of weakness are meant to make us stronger. It's a paradox, of course, how it is possible that we can be at our strongest when we are weak. But consider how these moments of weakness cause us to run to Him and allow Him to be our strength.

Such is the Christian life: a journey from strength to strength, from glory to glory, until we stand before Him face to face.

May your weakness lead you to His strength. May His strength lead you to His glory. May His glory shine ever brighter in you and through you until we appear before God in Zion.

day 13

THE GOSSAMER PRINCE

Twilight faded and dusk drew near, and since the sycamore had hurried her away, she hadn't yet trekked too far along the forest path. She asked herself if she should gather firewood, but hesitated when she realized she didn't have a fire to light it with. She shrugged.

I might as well gather some in case He sends light somehow.

Eventually, she had an ample supply of wood, so beneath a tree, she arranged a pile beside a bed of leaves. The moment she settled down to wait for light, darkness consumed the day and covered the forest.

She wondered where the light would come from, but remembered what He told her through the sycamore: His Word will light your path when it gets dark.

Determined not to let the darkness bother her, she shut her eyes. A passage in Jeremiah she didn't quite understand came to mind.

Faithless Israel is more righteous than unfaithful Judah.

What was the difference? She would rather be neither.

She wanted to be faithful to Him. Still, the passage bothered her until two other passages circled her mind.

> *The fear of the LORD is the beginning of knowledge... The fear of the LORD is the beginning of wisdom and knowledge of the Holy One is understanding.*

What does all this mean?

She opened her eyes, half-expecting to see darkness, half-expecting to see light.

Oh, me of little faith!

She rebuked herself, ashamed that she still doubted His ability to come through for her.

As her eyes opened, however, a rather amazing sight greeted her. A small young man, with a gossamer countenance and shining, translucent wings, settled on the ground beside her. She estimated his height to be as tall as the distance from her elbow to the tip of her forefinger. He wore a wreath of emerald leaves on his head. He smiled at her and glanced at the firewood. His smile turned into a big grin when he pointed at the wooden pile. She jolted in surprise when a brilliant fire suddenly blazed over the wood and dissipated the surrounding darkness.

He winked at her as he sat down on the ground and stared at the fire.

"I'm the Gossamer Prince, if you're wondering. I'd shake your hand, but I'm positive you can crush me with it, so a 'hello' would suffice."

So, she smiled and said, "Hello," to the winged gossamer prince.

VERSES FOR MEDITATION

The LORD said to me, "Faithless Israel is more righteous than unfaithful Judah.
Jeremiah 3:11

The fear of the LORD is the beginning of knowledge...
Proverbs 1:7

The fear of the Lord is the beginning of wisdom, and knowledge of the Holy One is understanding.
Proverbs 9:10

AUTHOR'S REFLECTIONS

He longs for a wholehearted bride. I like to think we long to be wholehearted in our pursuit of Him, but if you are anything like me, then to some extent, you have a divided heart. The way we spend our time and money, the way we struggle in our thought life, and the choices we make all reflect whether we are wholehearted.

We have seasons of wholeheartedness, but then we falter, we stumble, we fall. We talk about how we want to know Him and His will, but we also neglect our devotion to Him.

He understands what pulls us here and there, to and fro. He loves us still, but He also pines for our faithfulness, for us to love Him with everything we are.

May the fear of the Lord show us the way to wholeheartedness, so we can be undivided, wholly His.

day 14

THE UNFAITHFUL

*S*hould she ask him what on earth a gossamer prince was?

"It doesn't matter what I am! All that matters is I'm here. He sent me to light up all this—" his eyes scanned their surroundings "—well, darkness. He sends His love, though His love is always with you. His love endures when all things fail."

His words lifted her spirit like no other. At the idea of His mind containing thoughts of her, she gushed, "I love Him. I long to be with Him!"

The gossamer prince looked at her with a bittersweet expression on his small, handsome face.

"If only those I love can respond to my love the way you respond to His. Surely He delights in how you yearn for Him. I know I would if the one I love would yearn for me as you do and travel across a wilderness to find me as you are doing now." The sadness in his face broke her heart.

"What happened?" she asked.

"The woman I love was mine for a season. She used to love me, but a time came when she left me for another. She turned her back on me and broke my heart. The lovers she left me for broke her heart too. They couldn't love her or take care of her like I could, yet she ran after them. After a while, she returned to me. She professed her love for me. I accepted her, but when she is not with me, when she thinks I cannot see and cannot hear, she pursues pleasure with her former lovers behind my back. Which is worse? Her fickle-mindedness in abandoning me when she first left me? Or her treacherousness now that she has returned to me? Would you blame me if I cast her away? I love her, but I cannot live blind to her treachery."

Tears of compassion flowed down her cheeks as she listened to the prince's sad story. He, too, had tears running down his face. They wept together for a while before all became clear to her.

> Do we fear Him? Backslidden Israel was less guilty than Treacherous Judah. How many of us who profess our love to Him is like Judah? How many of us say we are for Him, but serve other idols before Him? We treat Him without the reverence He deserves.

She looked at the young prince whose heart ached for the one he loved, and though she knew the answer, she asked anyway, "Would you take her back?"

With a heart-breaking mixture of love and sadness in his eyes, he nodded and said, "Yes."

She smiled, heart-broken by his love. She wanted to assure him she would return, but how could she be certain his beloved would?

If only she realized how loved she was!

The sojourner's' thoughts shifted to a greater Love.

> If only our world realized how loved it is.

Manna

VERSES FOR MEDITATION

For God so loved the world that he gave his one and only Son, that whoever believes in him shall not perish but have eternal life.
John 3:16

This is how much God loved the world: He gave his Son, his one and only Son. And this is why: so that no one need be destroyed; by believing in him, anyone can have a whole and lasting life. God didn't go to all the trouble of sending his Son merely to point an accusing finger, telling the world how bad it was. He came to help, to put the world right again. Anyone who trusts in him is acquitted; anyone who refuses to trust him has long since been under the death sentence without knowing it. And why? Because of that person's failure to believe in the one-of-a-kind Son of God when introduced to him.
John 3:16-18 (MSG)

AUTHOR'S REFLECTIONS

His love for us is immense and unimaginable. In its greatness, it was worth the ultimate sacrifice. In this quest to follow Him, let's learn to daily soak in His love. We cannot bask in His love if we do not spend time with Him, the Source of true, unconditional love.

Is it too difficult to sacrifice our time? Is it too hard to sacrifice anything for one such as He? Scripture speaks of a great, almighty God, Who time and time again, wooed humanity into relationship with Him.

He is wooing us. He is wooing you. When will we lay down every idol, embrace the cross, and follow Him?

He has cleared the way. Come away with Him.

THE JUBILANT

The gossamer prince's eyes veiled innumerable sorrows, but as sure as pain existed, so did joy. When the last of the night's tears for his unrequited love hit the ground, a gem appeared where it had fallen.

She had never seen a treasure like it before, for it reflected greater light than the fire it mirrored.

Joy replaced the sorrow on the prince's face as he flew towards the gem. Picking it up, he easily lifted it above his head to show her. "Do you know what this means?" he exclaimed.

She smiled, shook her head, and worried that the gem, at least twice the size of his head, might fall on him.

"It's a promise! The Lover of Souls loves fulfilling His promises, and He is faithful in making them happen."

"That is true," she said. "But what is this a promise of?"

"Those who sow in tears will reap in joy! My beloved may not love me, but as sure as the sun rises, I know He will bring me someone who will." Sheer conviction pulled at the contours of his handsome face, and he made it seem like nothing could ever erase his smile. His eyes mirrored the sparkle of the brilliant gem in his hands. "Good things will come for us; so, be not dismayed, beautiful one. The Liar will try to discourage you as he has tried many times to discourage me, but we are a people of good courage! Oh, woman in the wilderness, don't you see? What treasures await you! He has a promise for me, and surely, He has a promise for you!"

Gem still lifted in the air, he danced around the fire. So enraptured was he in his jubilation, she hesitated to ask what begged asking. She cleared her throat.

He stopped short of his dance and laughed.

She didn't need to say anything. It seemed he already knew what was flitting in her mind.

What is His promise to me?

"Ah yes," he said. "Forgive me for being swept away by celebration. The gem reminded me if we only open our eyes, we discover much reason to celebrate." His wings carried him up in the air. He extended the gem toward her. She opened her hand, and he placed the gem on her palm. "Do not waver in your quest to find Him, because tonight, He reminds you He is a Rewarder of those who seek Him. Much trouble comes along the way, but take heart. He has overcome the world."

She held on to the gem, even as their eyes met, and the prince's joy overflowed to her. "Thank you," she said.

"He gave you a fire, a story, and a promise, beloved. It's everything you need for a night's peaceful rest. I shall see you again."

In a blink, he disappeared, but she was the farthest thing from alone, because His presence remained with her.

Manna

VERSES FOR MEDITATION

Not one of all the Lord's good promises to Israel failed; every one was fulfilled.
Joshua 21:45

Those who sow with tears will reap with songs of joy.
Psalm 126:5

And without faith it is impossible to please God, because anyone who comes to him must believe that he exists and that he rewards those who earnestly seek him.
Hebrews 11:6

"I have told you these things, so that in me you may have peace. In this world you will have trouble. But take heart! I have overcome the world."
John 16:33

AUTHOR'S REFLECTIONS

Have you ever received any of His promises or decided to obey Him only to wonder why things did not pan out as expected?

We often go through this world, aware of the troubles surrounding us, and — face it — each day has plenty of trouble, and there's more of it we'll encounter. But, His promises give us hope, because no matter what situation we find ourselves in, He is true to His Word.

Where we have sown in tears, we will reap in joy. Where we have seen trouble, if we seek Him, if we set our eyes on Him in faith, He will be our Rewarder. His Word says so.

We struggle through seasons of faltering, when we feel like we can't hold on to faith, but I pray He will give you the faith you need. Just like the woman in the story, may someone remind you that you can find joy in the wilderness, and that you and I are never alone.

day 16

THE STONE TROUBADOUR

She woke up to memories of the gossamer prince's laughter, and somehow, she didn't doubt he would soon find much reason to rejoice. After rising from the ground, she found her clothing cleaner than it had been the night before, as if untouched by the dirt she had slept on.

His mercies are new every morning,

a whisper in the wind reminded her. She watched the last of the fire's embers flicker away as sunlight immersed the forest. She basked in the warmth, saying a prayer of thanks to the Father of Lights as, between her fingers, she rolled the gem — the symbol of His promise. A good and perfect gift coming from a good Father.

Not long after she had left the campfire and had ventured deeper into the forest wilderness, her peace pointed her northbound, where His kingdom stood. She trekked further for a while until she heard lively music fill the air.

Someone plucked a stringed instrument somewhere ahead of her. As she drew closer, and the music grew louder, her heart raced with anticipation, eager to meet more of His creatures. A baritone voice sang to the merry stringed tune.

He is loved by many
Though she doesn't see
She's quite the fool
Oh, beloved Folly
If she won't make haste –

The song stopped as she approached a clearing in the forest, revealing a lake and a man with a lyre. He sat on a rock, and his feet dangled over the waters. Delight sparked in his eyes at the sight of her.

"You must be the sojourner!" he exclaimed. "The gossamer prince told me about you! Oh, the whispers about you! My, how great to see you!"

She didn't know what to make of the merry welcome, but his delight filled her heart with happiness.

"I'm the Troubadour, and I sing new songs. Songs of joy and songs that tell His stories. There's always a reason to sing. There's always a reason to praise."

She smiled at him. "It's good to meet you." She knelt on the ground by the pool and enjoyed a refreshing gulp of water.

He then tossed her a piece of bread after the drink quenched her thirst. "He wants you to have it."

She sat down. What wisdom would the Troubadour impart to her? When he plucked another tune, she blinked her eyes several times, because she realized the Troubadour was a creature of stone.

He beamed at her. "Why so surprised, sojourner?" His smile faded away. "Did He not say that should many grow silent, even stones will cry out His praise?"

She swallowed hard, understanding then the sadness in the song and the story, he began to play. And if only in her heart, and in a whisper, she chose to give the Lover of Souls praise.

Manna

VERSES FOR MEDITATION

The steadfast love of the Lord never ceases;
his mercies never come to an end;
they are new every morning;
great is your faithfulness.
Lamentations 3:22-23 (ESV)

Every good thing given and every perfect gift is from
above; it comes down from the Father of lights [the
Creator and Sustainer of the heavens], in whom there is
no variation [no rising or setting] or shadow cast by His
turning [for He is perfect and never changes].
James 1:17 (AMP)

But he said, "If they kept quiet, the stones would do it
for them, shouting praise."
Luke 19:40 (MSG)

AUTHOR'S REFLECTIONS

Songs of joy and praise are necessary to get through the wilderness. We can't get by without it. In wilderness seasons, where we are far from distractions, and we find ourselves away from sources of instant gratification, we can find many reasons to grumble and complain. The wilderness, however, is meant to teach us the discipline of praising Him no matter what our circumstances look like.

To hold on to His promises and praise Him by faith, and not by what we see, is a treasure in itself. In good and in bad, all of creation exists to give Him praise.

Do we praise Him in times of joy and in times of sorrow? Or do we forget He is the Father of Lights, the One faithful in giving us each morning and all the new mercies coming with it? Is He not the Giver of every good and perfect gift we've received? Is He not perfect in all of His ways?

And is He not worthy of our praise?

Praise Him.

day 17

THE ABSENCE OF PRAISE

The troubadour sang of a maiden who far too often forgot all her lover had done for her. Her lover, who once had found her in desolation and had taken her in, had clothed her with fine linen, and had adorned her with gold. He had given her a love like no other, had ignored her past, had restored her future, and had returned her dignity. Yet the moment she could stand on her own, she left him and ran after other lovers.

Such was the sorrow of the troubadour's song. As he plucked the last chord, a tear ran down his cheek. But as soon as the tear dropped from his chin, the troubadour once again found a reason to praise.

As she swallowed her morsel of bread, a longing stirred up in her soul. The desire almost seemed wrong, but it spoke to the deepest part of her.

He is worthy of my praise, but am I deserving of His? At the end of this journey, will I find Him saying, "Well done." Or will He tell me He never knew me and turn His back on me?

The yearning to know His mind and His heart grew so great in its magnitude, it overwhelmed her. How long was her journey going to take? His kingdom stood so distant, so unreachable.

She grasped the gem the gossamer prince had given her. She tried to remember His promises, but all she could think about were the troubadour's song and how she herself was as guilty as the maiden it mentioned.

He knows my inmost being more than I do. What darkness does He see there? He knows me. He sees me. Every motive. Every desire. Did I journey through this wilderness to seek Him out and find Him or am I only drawn by the treasures His kingdom offers?

The gem in her hand, once a promise of joy and great reward, lost its appeal.

What am I doing? Why am I here?

The question bubbled up from within her, begging her to ask: "Is He pleased with me?"

His song interrupted, the troubadour's eyes took on an expression, indecipherable.

"Does He like me?" she added.

The troubadour smiled. "That's not a question for me to answer, sojourner," he said in a tone meant for a child.

Before she could protest, the musician faded into the rock. The stone troubadour was no more. He left her soul longing to praise the Lover of Souls, but fearing she was unworthy of the journey she had determined to take.

And if only to find an answer to her question, 'Does He like me?', she wandered deeper into the wilderness.

Manna

VERSES FOR MEDITATION

*You have searched me, Lord,
and you know me.*
Psalm 139:1

*Search me, God, and know my heart;
test me and know my anxious thoughts.
See if there is any offensive way in me,
and lead me in the way everlasting.*
Psalm 139:23-24

*His master replied, 'Well done, good and faithful
servant! You have been faithful with a few things; I will
put you in charge of many things. Come and share your
master's happiness!'*
Matthew 25:21,23

AUTHOR'S REFLECTIONS

How many times have you decided or done something
and wondered later if it was what He wanted you to
do?

To hold a full perspective of who we are before
Him is rare. A lot of times, we are not even aware,
but He knows why we are on this journey. If we are in
this for the right reasons, if we are intent on pursuing
Him, we long to hear His approval and praise. The last
thing we want is to reach the end of our wilderness
and find we have wasted the experience. Through it
all, we murmured and grumbled and didn't discover a
deeper, more intimate knowledge of Him.

Being in the wilderness is a journey of hope where
we go through barrenness wanting to birth something
of the Spirit and not of the flesh. With hope comes

peace. When life shakes our peace, it is a time to pause and reflect on how to fight for our peace, because we cannot go on without it. We allow Him to search us, to remove whatever keeps our eyes from the reason we're in this journey to begin with: Know Him. Be with Him. Delight in Him.

To share in His happiness.

day 18

THE MIST OF THE ABYSS

With every step, her heart grew heavier. Questions she couldn't find answers to cluttered her mind. She dragged her feet with every step, each one feeling more of a battle than the last.

Aware of her weakness, her hunger and her thirst, she found her bread and water unsatisfying. She questioned whether she could take another step, much more reach the end of the wilderness, but she pressed on and remembered when one wiser than her admonished her.

*Press toward the mark for the prize of
the high calling...*

Every time it felt as if her knees would give way beneath her, she gritted her teeth and took another step forward.

Why was this so difficult? She fought the urge to pity herself, for she didn't wish to dishonor Him by thinking herself a victim in a journey she had taken of her own free will.

Hope surged within her when she saw a clearing ahead. Could it be? Could it be the end of this wilderness and the start of His kingdom?

Her every step grew harder, almost as if the air itself kept her from her destination, but despite the opposition, she walked on. Her hope grew with every successful, albeit painful, step.

When she reached the clearing, her knees collapsed beneath her at the sight awaiting her. Despair took over.

He doesn't like me! He doesn't want me here! Many are called, but few are chosen. I am not among the chosen. If I am, then shouldn't He clear the way for me?

Yet, right before her was the sight of a distant kingdom and a deep, dark abyss standing in the way of her reaching the One she loved.

Tears streamed down her cheeks as discouragement took over. She stared into the bottomless chasm standing between the edge of the forest and the rest of the wilderness. A dark mist rising from the pit covered her like a blanket attempting to seep into her skin and darken her soul.

Her palms pressed against the ground, and her knees dug into the dirt. Her spirit battled as she did the one thing she could do to fight back the mist. She pried her eyes away from the abyss and focused on the kingdom of shining light. With what started as a song whispered, she worshiped.

> *Though He slay me, yet will I trust Him.*

I will worship. I am called to be here, to worship Him in the desert. That much I know for sure.

So with every ounce of strength left in her, she raised her hands in the air and surrendered. As she sang in sweet abandon, the abyss in front of her remained, but the mist cleared. She was free.

Manna

Verses for Meditation

I press toward the mark for the prize of the high calling of God in Christ Jesus.
Philippians 3:14 (KJV)

Though he slay me, yet will I trust in him: but I will maintain mine own ways before him.
Job 13:15 (KJV)

Then say to him, 'The Lord, the God of the Hebrews, has sent me to say to you: Let my people go, so that they may worship me in the wilderness...'
Exodus 7:16

Author's Reflections

Despair. Hopelessness. Discouragement.

A sojourner in the wilderness finds these feelings familiar. In our walk with God, we've experienced one or all of these. Deep, meaningless, seemingly unending. Because of our human nature, we question and doubt.

Did He call us? Does He want us?

As much as we long for His answers, sometimes, He stays silent. With His silence comes emptiness — a hunger and a thirst begging to be filled. These moments in life cultivate in us a hope, a discipline, and a faith we can't gain anywhere else.

In the middle of your trials, when all you have is a tiny shred of hope that you are His and you are chosen, are you still able to worship? Are you still able to lift those hands in surrender, and tell Him that in Him, you have placed your trust? We must learn to worship Him in the wilderness if we are to make it through.

Do so, and let the despair clear.
No matter what's going on, we worship.

day 19

EAGLE'S WINGS

Joy welled up from the depths of her soul to the utterances of her lips as she sang song after song with all her might. After she had spent all her strength — her throat sore — she let her laughter fill the silence. The weight in her heart fell away. The chaos in her mind came to a perfect calm.

In the silence, she waited.

Gradually, understanding came to her as she quieted her soul. She waited for deliverance and strength.

She opened her eyes and found the abyss still there, but she barely noticed it, because she now perceived with new eyes. The kingdom felt far closer than it did before.

As she waited, the mist cleared and uncovered the abyss, which seemed far less threatening than it had been when she had first seen it. She could tell in her heart there would be battles ahead, but she held no doubt she'd be able to cross the abyss. Her strength returned, and she remembered the promise in His letter: her strength would rise as she waited upon Him.

She rose to her feet, fists clenched. One word echoed in her mind: Glory. His presence embraced her and filled her with the courage she needed.

With shoulders squared and eyes lifted, a smile appeared on her face.

He is a Shield about me, my Glory, the Lifter of my head.

A loud flutter of wings and the cry of an eagle echoed across the skies. Before she could comprehend what was happening, her feet lifted off the ground, and the eagle carried her away, over the abyss and onto the other side.

She heard an anguished and violent war cry from the depths of the dark pit. She shuddered, knowing she couldn't reach the kingdom of light without a fight, but her decree was victory.

Her feet landed on the ground. Steady. The powerful sound of the eagle's wings faded as the invisible bird disappeared, leaving only a single feather to remind her of Whom her strength was coming from.

She would need the reminder in the days ahead. Her trek through the wilderness would still span quite a distance, but she contained within her renewed strength and wild anticipation over the adventure ahead.

Verses for Meditation

But they that wait upon the Lord shall renew their strength; they shall mount up with wings as eagles; they shall run, and not be weary; and they shall walk, and not faint.
Isaiah 40:31 (KJV)

But you, O Lord, are a shield about me, my glory, and the lifter of my head.
Psalm 3:3 (ESV)

Author's Reflections

In a world full of noise and distraction, waiting on the Lord is one of the hardest disciplines a Christian has to learn. The wilderness, however, is a great place to cultivate this spiritual practice.

We grow in spirit when we get silent before Him and wait for Him to do as He will. When we wait on the Lord, it is an act of surrender, an acknowledgment of our dependency on Him. It is our way of setting our eyes on Him, the ultimate prize. It enables us to refocus, to reconfigure our mindsets so we are looking towards His kingdom instead of our circumstances.

I don't know what your wilderness looks like. Mine often has seasons of solitude, sprinkled with a reserved amount of fellowship. In my wilderness seasons, I'm tempted to run towards technology or entertainment or people to fill that abyss within me, but I have found that none satisfies like Him. I crave His presence and ask Him as Moses once did in the wilderness, "Oh God, show me now Your glory."

day 20

HIS OPEN HAND

*S*he hadn't expected the landscape that greeted her on the other side of the abyss. Where she had expected arid deserts, she found green grass beneath her feet and fresh air filling her lungs. A cool breeze caressed her skin, like an assuring whisper of good things to come.

Her spirit shifted, as if favor in battle had just tipped within her, and her spirit gained ground on her flesh.

She walked forward with a smile on her face and peace in her soul. Her joy spilled over when she found still waters in the form of a quiet pool. She knelt on the ground and cupped water into her hands and quenched her thirst. The water, like medicine, brought healing and restoration to her soul.

He loves me! My Guide and my Shield brought me here!

Laughter filled her heart and spilled out of her lips. She knew this was a momentary reprieve, a time to catch her breath, but she also feared nothing. Even knowing all her journey's dangers and all the reasons to falter, His presence within her assured her nothing could harm her.

With her thirst satiated, she lay on the grass, stared at the clear blue sky, and relished the exhilarating sense of being alive. She then heard it. Footsteps drew near. When she sat up, her heart leapt. Was He a vision? A figment of her imagination brought about by a deep longing?

He Who loved her like no other, opened his hand, scarred by His love for her, and extended it to her. An invitation to be with Him before she ventured once again into the depths of her wilderness.

For a moment, reverence filled her, almost as if His touch scared her, but love and joy overpowered the fear. Coming to her senses, she reached for His open hand, and they walked together by the still waters. Both quiet and content to be in each other's company, they lingered in the presence of Love.

Manna

Verses for Meditation

The Lord is my Shepherd [to feed, to guide and to shield me], I shall not want. He lets me lie down in green pastures; He leads me beside the still and quiet waters. He refreshes and restores my soul (life); He leads me in the paths of righteousness for His name's sake.
Psalm 23:1-3 (AMP)

*You open Your hand
And satisfy the desire of every living thing.*
Psalm 145:16 (NKJV)

Author's Reflections

Encounter. Nothing satisfies more than those sweet, intimate, personal encounters we have with Jesus. If you have spent significant time in your pursuit of Him, then you've had one of these. Moments when you are fully aware He is right there with you. We live for times like these, when we experience His manifest presence, and if we could only linger! If we could only stay there forever! It's a foretaste of heaven. A mountaintop experience. Here, we encounter Him in a deeper and greater way than any other part of our wilderness journey.

Wherever you are in your relationship with God, I pray you have one of these encounters. I pray you enjoy those moments when you want nothing more than to linger in His presence, held by His hand, surrounded by His love.

May these moments restore you and give you strength for the journey ahead. We crave these moments. We need these moments. May He grant it to you and me, encounters with Him that will carry us through as we follow Him wherever He may lead.

day 21

DELIGHT

*S*he wanted to tell Him about countless things — questions in her mind, cries of her heart — but she couldn't string together the right words to say. She dared a glance His way and longed to see His face, but she couldn't. His hand held hers, but a veil of light hid His countenance from her. In the absence of her words, His presence and touch satisfied her. She longed to linger there forever, but her journey through the wilderness was far from over, and this glorious rendezvous prepared her for what's ahead.

"IT'S TIME, BELOVED," He said.

"Time?" she asked.

"TIME TO LEAVE WHAT CAME BEFORE AND PRESS ON TOWARD WHAT LIES AHEAD. THIS IS A TIME FOR NEW THINGS. A TIME TO BEGIN AGAIN. WHATEVER HELD YOU BACK BEFORE CAN NO LONGER HOLD YOU BACK NOW. YOU NEED TO LEAVE THEM BY THE WAYSIDE."

For a moment, His words confused her. Was she not in this journey? Were there still things she hadn't surrendered to Him?

Did I not leave everything behind? Did I not venture into this wilderness with only His Word to sustain me?

He gave her a smile one would give to a child who had yet to learn many things. "I HAVE GONE BEFORE YOU, BELOVED. I HAVE CLEARED THE WAY. THERE WILL BE WARFARE AHEAD, BUT NO LONGER WILL YOU FACE DEAD ENDS AND OBSTACLES. THE WAY IS CLEAR. YOU WILL EXPERIENCE NEITHER THIRST NOR HUNGER. I WILL SUSTAIN YOU. WHAT YOU fiRST WENT THROUGH IN THE WILDERNESS IS NOT WHAT YOU WILL GO THROUGH IN THIS NEXT STAGE. ASK FOR HELP, AND IT WILL COME WITH NO DELAY. IT WILL ARRIVE IN ITS PERFECT TIME."

Speechless, she tried to record every word He had spoken in her mind and hoped she would remember when she needed to.

"DO YOU TRUST ME, MY LOVE?"

"Yes," she answered. "I want to trust You. Help me do that." The moment the words came out of her mouth, she sensed His delight spill over her. A prayer she uttered so many times before rushed back to her: "Let Your heart be my heart. Let Your thoughts be my thoughts."

And in that moment, she realized she was the reason for His delight. That knowledge became her delight as well, and it flowed into experience, for she learned yet another dimension of what it meant to rejoice in Him.

So, even when His manifest presence could no longer be sensed, His glory lingered in the atmosphere — even more so, in her heart. She carried His delight with her, and basked in the knowledge that she was His desire, and He was hers.

Manna

VERSES FOR MEDITATION

Do not remember the former things,
Or ponder the things of the past.
"Listen carefully, I am about to do a new thing,
Now it will spring forth;
Will you not be aware of it?
I will even put a road in the wilderness,
Rivers in the desert.
Isaiah 43:18-19 (AMP)

Delight yourself in the Lord,
And He will give you the desires and petitions of your
heart.
Psalm 37:4 (AMP)

AUTHOR'S REFLECTIONS

A shift happens somewhere in our walk through the wilderness. We can expect things won't always be the way it was. There's a tipping point, a transition, a change that becomes a catalyst to us getting closer to our land of promise.

We have plenty of ground to cover in our journey. It may take longer than expected, but He has promised to give us what we need to walk on. Consider it a transition to a new level. It's possible the challenges we face are not just different, but harder. A different level means new, more powerful foes, but the initial stages of the wilderness served as preparation for this. He did not bring us here unprepared, and should we lack anything for the rest of the journey, He has promised to give us what we need.

One of our greatest weapons in this season is the act of delighting in Him, being in His presence, and allowing Him to satisfy our needs and longings. At this point of our journey, it is important for us to trust He is Who He says He is. Then, we can anticipate what lies ahead, because we can expect we are about to see God move in ways we've never experienced before. Praise God!

day 22

RUDE AWAKENINGS

*S*he had expected the awareness of His presence to linger with her for the greater part of the journey. It didn't take long for her to discover how wrong she was.

Lying down in green meadows, she woke up to find the sun's rays stinging her skin. She knelt up, disoriented. True to His word, He had prepared a way for her to follow. A stone path led her to her destination, but she couldn't see the end of it.

How long will this journey take?

Her shoulders sagged. Looking around her, she saw nothing but an endless path winding through grass-covered hills. She felt weak, but before a sense of apprehension could take over, she applied what she had already learned. She took the love letter from her pouch, read the words of assurance written there, and waited for His strength in her to arise.

When she opened her eyes, she still felt weak.

It's not supposed to be this way. He promised it wouldn't be the same. He promised I wouldn't hunger or thirst.

Disheartened, she didn't even want to rise from where she knelt. She took a deep breath and shook her head, hoping to shake the frustration away. Once again, she shut her eyes and tried to recall her encounter with Him. "I trust You," she said. "You are true to Your Word."

"Do you have a habit of talking to yourself?" A small, high-pitched female voice made her jolt.

She opened her eyes. A winged creature, similar to the gossamer prince, flew at a height parallel to the woman's face. Hands planted on her waist, the winged woman looked irritated for reasons only she seemed to know.

"I wasn't talking to myself. I was talking to—"

"Someone who isn't here. My name is Folly. I'm here to make sure you have sustenance on this journey of yours."

"Who sent you?"

"Those higher than me. Those who control my fate. I long to be free, woman! Free! For the life of me, I can't understand why you would do something like this, go on a journey like this." Folly shook her tiny head and blabbered what sounded wise at first, foolish on second thought.

The flighty little wisp waved her hands in the air. Fruit and milk appeared on the ground, but the woman was so fascinated by her newfound acquaintance, she forgot her hunger. That was until Folly stopped ranting and gave her a pointed look. "Well? Aren't you going to eat?"

She whispered thanks to her Beloved for the food before taking a bite from an apple.

"What are you thanking Him for?" Folly harrumphed. "I'm the one who brought you the food."

She didn't know what to say, but it seemed Folly wasn't interested in listening to her, anyway.

"You really believe He loves you, huh? You're a fool, woman. Listen because I'm about to give you a rude awakening."

Manna

Verses for Meditation

Good friend, take to heart what I'm telling you;
collect my counsels and guard them with your life.
Tune your ears to the world of Wisdom;
set your heart on a life of Understanding.
Proverbs 2:1-2 (MSG)

Blessed is the one
who does not walk in step with the wicked
or stand in the way that sinners take
or sit in the company of mockers,
but whose delight is in the law of the Lord,
and who meditates on his law day and night.
Psalm 1:1-2

I have given them your word and the world has hated
them, for they are not of the world any more than I am
of the world. My prayer is not that you take them out of
the world but that you protect them from the evil one.
John 17:14-15

Author's Reflections

It's likely you've been in the company of mockers before. They are those who scorn you for your belief, persecute you for your faith, and question you for the stances you take. They love the world and refuse to understand what it is like to follow God.

It may surprise you, but some of them may even be Christians.

I doubt you are taking this journey in complete solitude, away from all mankind. It may already be a challenge for you to find enough time and quiet to be alone, draw away from people, and seek Him.

In this season, it's important to be around people who understand and support your journey. It's not the time to allow scornful mockers to surround you. If you are, however, among such company and can't draw away from them, it's even more important to lend an ear to His voice. This is a time to avoid foolishness and set your heart towards insight and understanding.

Perhaps the mockers you have — however not-ideal they are — surround you for a reason. Incline yourself to Him and ask Him how He can use them to teach you His ways. He called us to be in the world, not of it, and part of being in this world is being among those who are of it. God brought these people in our lives for a reason. He may even use them to bless us. Now, let's ask Him how we can bless and love them, so they too may know the off-the-beaten track of the narrow path.

THE LOGIC OF FOLLY

*S*he sat on the grass and ate in silence as Folly ranted. "Everyone acts like the gossamer prince is so perfect. They keep saying he loves me, and they paint me as this wicked villain who broke his heart. They don't know what it's like to be me! And that dratted troubadour, always singing songs about this lovelorn prince and his unfaithful beloved. No one knows what I've been through!" Folly emphasized the end of her every sentence with a kick in the air. Her wings carried her mid-air as she spoke, her words emphasized by animated hand gestures and exaggerated facial expressions.

The woman tilted her head to the side, swallowed a choice cut of meat, and sipped a drink of milk. "What have you been through, Folly?"

"Meaningless, everything is meaningless! It's toil and bitterness and misery and heartache. I just want to be happy you see, but he loves me, he says. What he doesn't tell everyone is his love requires me to change. What kind of love is that? How is love unconditional if I have to give myself up to get it?"

"I don't think—"

"Don't you dare defend him! Everyone in this wilderness does. I'm the wicked one, and he's the good one! Well, forget good! I don't want to be good. I want to be happy."

"Well, are you?" the woman asked.

"No, because he's always... there. Everywhere I go, everyone speaks of him. They sing the troubadour's songs, and when living creatures somehow manage to be silent, even the earth itself talks about this love the prince has for me. I just want him to leave me alone."

"Hasn't he? I don't see the gossamer prince here, so it seems like he's left you to do as you please."

"So he's abandoned me! How is that love? If he loves me, why isn't he chasing me? His love is a trap with so many strings attached! Why on earth should I be faithful to him?"

Folly continued her rant and anyone who listened could tell nothing the gossamer prince did would satisfy her, not until she herself could learn how to be loved.

The woman rushed to finish her meal, eager to leave the company of the angry winged creature, but when she returned to the path onwards, Folly kept her company.

Verses for Meditation

"Meaningless! Meaningless!"
says the Teacher.
"Utterly meaningless!
Everything is meaningless."
Ecclesiastes 1:2

"... because the Lord disciplines the one he loves,
and he chastens everyone he accepts as his son."
Endure hardship as discipline; God is treating you as
his children. For what children are not disciplined by
their father? If you are not disciplined—and everyone
undergoes discipline—then you are not legitimate, not
true sons and daughters at all.
Hebrews 12:6-8

Author's Reflections

The wise writer of Ecclesiastes spoke of the madness of human folly, which runs after pleasure and seeks one's happiness above all. It wants a love that permits whatever pleases, despite the destruction it can cause.

Love, however, does not sit back and watch us destroy ourselves. True love never gives up fighting for us, saving us from our own misdoings, even when we continue to push it away.

We've said many times before the wilderness is about discipline. It's about learning to trust that He is allowing us to go through the hardship, not because He's punishing us, but because He loves us. It's the equipping of our characters to receive and handle more of His glory.

I doubt any of us will say we enjoy being disciplined, but it is part of the process of transformation. It is part of the process of learning how to rule and reign by His side, and how to have the character to steward that authority well. Though folly may say otherwise, we don't have to change to earn His love. Instead, he loves us, and that is what changes us. His love transforms us to become vessels of glory.

May discipline silence folly, may His love compel you to walk on, and may He give you grace to praise and rejoice even in discipline.

day 24

THE PLEASURES OF FOLLY

For every yard the woman progressed along the path, she heard at least one complaint from Folly, who verbalized one too many grievances against the gossamer prince.

The sojourner recalled the expression on the prince's face when he first spoke to her about Folly. What did the prince find to love in this whiny little creature?

"You say you want to be happy, Folly. What exactly will make you happy? Do you know?"

"Freedom! I long to be free to do whatever I want."

"And what do you want?"

"I hope to experience all the pleasures this world has to offer! Imagine living for one pleasure after another, free to choose, free to just give in without having others judge you for it. What a world that would be! Of course, a world like that can never be as long as the likes of him exist!"

The sojourner winced at the memory of a time when she lived for such pleasure. How futile it all was, for she remained an empty shell, clamoring for the next wave of pleasure. She longed to leave her former life behind. She felt sorry for her companion because Folly seemed blind to the love she exchanged for pleasures unable to satisfy in the long run.

"Why are you doing this again?" Folly asked. "Why are you taking this insane journey?"

"I'm seeking the One I love, the One Who loves me."

Folly grimaced. "Why doesn't He seek you instead?"

"He already did. He drew me to this journey after He pursued me and loved me. I long to experience more of His love."

"Why?"

The woman searched her heart, soul and mind for an answer, and the one word she could think of was, "Pleasure — I am after the pleasure of being with Him. Folly, when you love someone, it becomes a pleasure to be with them, serve them, make them happy. You delight in their delight, desire what they desire."

Folly stopped short of her flight. She bobbed in the air. A frown formed on her small face. "Bah!" She exclaimed. "Sounds like sentimental nonsense. I don't understand you at all."

The woman sighed as they walked on.

I fear you might never understand. What loss, Folly. Your temporal pleasures can't compare to the eternal pleasure my Beloved offers.

Though her heart grieved for Folly, she walked on, more determined than ever to find in His presence, the fullness of joy.

Manna

VERSES FOR MEDITATION

*You make known to me the path of life;
in your presence there is fullness of joy;
at your right hand are pleasures forevermore.*
Psalm 16:11 (ESV)

*This is how God showed his love among us: He sent
his one and only Son into the world that we might
live through him. This is love: not that we loved God,
but that he loved us and sent his Son as an atoning
sacrifice for our sins.*
1 John 4:9-10

AUTHOR'S REFLECTIONS

Sometimes, we have to exchange legitimate pleasures for His glorious eternal ones. This may feel like we're giving up our own happiness to seek Him and His highest will for our lives.

We have seasons where we enter fasts — from food, from social media, from games, from anything distracting us from Him — so that we can put Him first in our lives.

This is not the way of folly, and not the way of the world, but this is the path to His sanctuary where He demonstrates the fullness of His joy.

Is His love and sacrifice for us not worth it? Can we not choose to "sacrifice" a little of our time, our appetites, our sources of temporary happiness to pursue a love such as His?

We're in this journey together, so I'm assuming the answer to that would be "Yes". May we daily renew our commitment to pursue God, and may He fill our hearts with anticipation even as we meditate on His promise that those who seek will indeed find.

THE TEMPTATION OF FOLLY

To endure Folly's incessant ranting, the woman hummed a song of praise. She smiled as she paid attention to the scenery surrounding the stone path. She noticed the clear skies and the vibrant flowers. Her ears tuned in to the chirps of different birds.

The variety and the multitude of flora and fauna surrounding her in the wilderness stunned her. How didn't she notice them before? Had they always been there?

What wonders we miss when we get too wrapped up in our own thoughts and troubles!

She caught sight of a hummingbird flitting about — a picture of one without a care in the world.

"Are you even listening?" Folly hovered in front of her face.

"No." She didn't want to lie. "Sorry. The scenery distracted me. It's breath-taking, is it not?"

"I guess." Folly crossed her arms and frowned.

"Why do you remain in this journey with me, Folly? You appear to want to be somewhere else or with someone else."

"I'm headed in the same direction. I'll go my own way soon enough."

Not long after, they came upon a forked road — one narrow, one wide. The stone path led to the narrow one which winded on to a dark wood. Meanwhile, the wide path ended on a concrete road that led to what looked like a small settlement — a village of sorts.

"Finally!" Folly exclaimed. "We have a bed to sleep in and some civilized company."

The woman took a deep breath. What she would give for a warm bed, a hot bath, and a steaming cup of any soothing drink! However, she knew which way to go, and she was about to follow the stone path when Folly tugged at her hair.

"Are you dumb?" the winged one asked.

"He promised a voice will tell me which way to go."

"And you're hearing voices now? You are mad!"

The woman paused. Was she hearing His voice? Was this the path He cleared out for her? Would He really mind if she wandered for a night, or two, at most?

"Come on." Folly tilted her head to the side. "Come with me, woman. One night. If He loves you, He'll understand. He won't mind. There's nothing wrong with straying away from the path. I know you're famished. There'll be a hot meal, a warm bed, anything you can ask for."

The promise of comfort led her away from where her heart knew she had to go. Her mind rationalized her decision, and she walked towards a village of compromise.

"Great!" Folly approved. "You're not as boring as you seem, after all."

They were about to approach the wide metal gate that led to the settlement when something made her stop in her tracks. No. A Voice not of the heart, soul, nor mind spoke to her. "You mustn't," it said.

The temptation to ignore the Voice was almost too much to fight — especially for one as weary as her. Almost.

"What are you doing? Let's go!" Folly beckoned.

The woman shook her head. "I can't."

"Why not?"

"I'm afraid."

"Of what?"

"Of settling for less than the best He offers. Thank you for the company, Folly, but we must go our separate ways."

Folly threw her hands in the air and mumbled

something about what a waste of time the sojourner was. With a final wave of goodbye, she sped towards the settlement.

Meanwhile, the woman turned back, glad she received the grace to obey, dreading how long she had to walk alone.

Manna

VERSES FOR MEDITATION

Whether you turn to the right or to the left, your ears will hear a voice behind you, saying, "This is the way; walk in it."
Isaiah 30:21

Fear of the LORD is the foundation of true wisdom. All who obey his commandments will grow in wisdom. Praise him forever!
Psalm 111:10 (NLT)

Enter through the narrow gate. For wide is the gate and broad is the road that leads to destruction, and many enter through it. But small is the gate and narrow the road that leads to life, and only a few find it.
Matthew 7:13-14

AUTHOR'S REFLECTIONS

The path leading to God can often be a lonely one. The further we go, it seems the lonelier it gets. He made us for fellowship and community, to learn how to love one another and thrive as the Body of Christ. During wilderness seasons, we may not be among a healthy community of Christ-followers. It's even possible our Christian community doesn't understand what our wilderness season is like. However, God can provide people and leaders who've been through wilderness seasons. They are there for you, praying for you and cheering you on, but they understand too that the wilderness, most of the time, is a journey between you and God.

It's a personal journey that draws us toward a God Who wants to reveal Himself to us in a way unique to our personal relationship with Him. These are the moments we spend extended times waiting on Him, seeking Him, yearning to find Him.

We're taking a hard and narrow path. Few have walked down this road, but we take it anyway, because He led us here. He drew us here. He will meet us here, and when the enemy tempts us to stray, we have the voice of the Holy Spirit reminding us where to go. The fear of the Lord rises within us and establishes Godly wisdom.

Here, we learn to listen to the holy fear that stops us and the sacred Voice that guides us.

day 26

THE PATH OF LONELINESS

She missed Folly's chatter. As much as she didn't like hearing all the rants and complaints, having company was nice. The starkness of the path she had chosen magnified her solitude. She was in this on her own. A vagrant soul longing, pining, yearning for a kingdom beyond.

Eyes downcast and heart heavy, she kept walking. She didn't quite understand why she was suddenly so overcome by loneliness. Hadn't she taken this journey on her own to begin with? Was this not a personal pilgrimage, one between her and her Beloved? Why then did she so long for companionship?

Night drew nigh, and the path had no end in sight. How long was she supposed to be alone?

Doubt crept in. Subtle. Not as obvious as the all-too-familiar slither. Based on her circumstances, it seemed so logical, so natural to doubt. She had forgotten how He had always sent someone or something to sustain her. She searched for firewood and wandered away, far enough to find wood, but close enough to keep sight of the path.

Once satisfied with the pile she had found, she set camp on the wayside, close to the path. And then she waited.

She knew upon passing through the abyss, things would be different. He would no longer send the gossamer prince to make a fire for her. She stared at the pile of firewood, her anger growing as dusk became night and darkness covered the landscape.

Nothing. No light, no help, no creature sent to conjure fire, quench her hunger, tell her stories, or give her company. Just her, a pile of wood, darkness, and silence.

Now what? Why did I get myself into this predicament?

She had obeyed and chosen the narrow path even when the wide gate seemed so enticing. Her shoulders trembled. Tears rushed down her cheeks. She wanted to give up and turn back, but to where? To the wide gate? To where she had come from? She had already gone so far into the wilderness, so much closer to Him. She had gone past the point of no return, and now, she felt stuck, but the path of loneliness was her road to take, and there was no going back.

VERSES FOR MEDITATION

We proclaim to you what we have seen and heard, so that you also may have fellowship with us. And our fellowship is with the Father and with his Son, Jesus Christ.
1 John 1:3

Jesus replied: "'Love the Lord your God with all your heart and with all your soul and with all your mind.' This is the first and greatest commandment.
Matthew 22:37-38

AUTHOR'S REFLECTIONS

God made us for fellowship. We need to be with people, if we are to learn to love them as Christ commands us to. It's about our fellowship with our Creator.

God could've made Adam and Eve one after the other, but He chose not to. He made Adam first because He wanted to establish man's relationship with God before establishing his relationship with the woman. Sometimes, we find it hard to wrap our hearts and minds around this truth, but in the wilderness, we need to come face-to-face with this.

Does He come first? When stripped of everything, is He more than enough? In our clamoring for Him to fulfill the desires of our hearts, do we find joy and satisfaction in Him?

The wilderness can often be a place of great loneliness, because this is where we empty ourselves, so He can fill us with His glory, His greatness, His wonder. Before the filling could happen, however, the emptying must first occur. That process can be painful, because it strips so much from us. Sometimes we question Him, question why we had chosen this path. Is He really good? Why does it feel this way? Where is He?

While living on earth, we will face moments when there are no quick answers, no instant solutions. We obey, but He doesn't reward us. We go to bed wondering if He really cares, but even as we lay our heads to rest, we remember and hold on to His Word. He is with us, so we pray. We pray for Him to give us the faith to get us through the dark night because we know the morning brings light. And tomorrow, we walk on. We love Him still, and we trust we will receive our just reward.

day 27

THE WOMAN'S END

She woke up with her bones aching, muscles straining, breath heaving. Her dreamless sleep brought her no assurances of His presence. There had been no fire, no food, no water. All she had was her satchel, His letter, the prince's gem, and the eagle's feather.

None of it seemed enough. She tried to remember all the good things that had happened in her journey, all the things that had kept her going, but none lifted the weight in her heart. She wanted to lie by the wayside, next to her fireless pile of wood, unmoving.

And there it was again. Her old friend, the slither came with its lies coiling itself around her heart, vocalizing words she was already telling herself.

> He abandoned you. You obeyed Him,
> gave your life to Him, sought Him in
> this miserable quest of yours, and in
> exchange, He abandoned you.

> Is this Love?

Self-pity attacked her soul, and she forced herself to push back at the slither and rise from her position of defeat.

He will never leave me nor forsake me.

The slither laughed.

> Fool, He already has. Where is He? He left
> you alone. You should've gone with Folly.

Her shoulders shook as she prayed for a miracle to change the hunger in her belly and the loneliness of her journey, but nothing happened.

Languishing, she remained still as lie after lie after lie assailed her, all of which seemed true.

Abandoned, starving and miserable, she took a deep breath and hoped it would ease the weight in her heart, but it didn't. She tried to stand up, but her knees felt weak, her skin felt cold, her heart felt heavy, and her soul felt empty.

I can't anymore.

She loved Him with her every breath, and she knew she couldn't quit, but she couldn't go on any longer either, so she sat and waited.

She had reached her end, and she wasn't sure how to begin again.

Verses for Meditation

*The Lord himself goes before you and will be with you;
he will never leave you nor forsake you. Do not be
afraid; do not be discouraged.*
Deuteronomy 31:8

*You're blessed when you're at the end of your rope.
With less of you there is more of God and his rule.*
Matthew 5:3 (MSG)

Author's Reflections

One of the most painful parts of journeying through
the wilderness is reaching the end of our strength
where we find ourselves with nothing left to keep
going. We went through the ringer and reached the
point where we just can't take it anymore. We have
reached the end of what we can handle on our own
strength, and if He doesn't come through for us, we
won't be able to go on.

I don't know if you've ever been at this point in
your walk with God — days when getting out of bed is
a struggle. Every smile becomes a triumph because it
takes so much out of you to do it.

You just can't. Not anymore.

Your heart for God hasn't changed. He is good
and worthy. He is Love. You do not regret taking the
journey, and you cannot envision yourself ever turning
back, but you cannot envision yourself continuing
either.

Don't be discouraged. God sees you. No matter
what lies the enemy tells you, know God's eyes are on
you. He is moving on your behalf — perhaps not in the
way you want or expect, but He is moving.

You may not see it right now, but He is carrying you. Glory to glory to glory. In due time, you will recognize His fingerprint in it all.

day 28

THE CHORUS

Whether she was there for minutes, hours, or days didn't seem to matter. She pulled her knees to her chest and stared at the space in front of her and stopped trying to process the chaos ravaging her mind and soul.

She craved for renewal, but how to attain it was beyond her, so she waited. She waited at this point — a stalemate between her restless soul and trusting spirit.

Until finally, it happened. Indecipherable at first, barely audible, but the sound rose to a spine-tingling crescendo that saturated her sinews and seeped into the very marrow of her bones. She heard voices. A multitude of voices, powerful and urgent. Almost violent. The voices filled the entire forest, like a shield engulfing her, a weapon preparing the way for her.

Prayers.

Many who desired to see her succeed pleaded to the heavens. Some who were well-acquainted with the hardships of her journey declared words of encouragement. Others, who also longed to become sojourners, prayed she'd be able to pave an easier way for them to reach His kingdom.

The wondrous chorus uplifted her heart like no other. She wasn't alone!

Her eyes cleared. And though her heart remained heavy, her mind stilled for but one moment before she picked up on it. Something snapped inside her as her thoughts realigned and her focus shifted.

She knew what awaited her at the end of the wilderness. It wasn't what she had hoped for or what she had dreamed of. His ways and thoughts were higher than hers, but in the disappointment, she could smile.

He was about to do a new thing — something she never thought possible, and if it took her disappointment to make it happen, then she would gladly pay the price.

The old has gone. The new has come.

Using all the strength she could muster, she rose to her feet and stared at her pile of wood. A fire sparked.

She smiled, knowing this time...

...the fire came from within her.

Manna

VERSES FOR MEDITATION

Therefore, since we are surrounded by such a great cloud of witnesses, let us throw off everything that hinders and the sin that so easily entangles. And let us run with perseverance the race marked out for us
Hebrews 12:1

Therefore, if anyone is in Christ, he is a new creation. [a] The old has passed away; behold, the new has come.
2 Corinthians 5:17

AUTHOR'S REFLECTIONS

Remember when you're in the wilderness: you are not alone.

Our seasons in the wilderness may be solitary journeys forcing us to linger in His presence. People around us may not understand, but the fact remains: we are not alone.

Wilderness seasons can be more of an internal battle, rather than an external one, so we must be intentional in seeking help from those who have gone before us. We must remember when things get tough, we can ask others to join us in our struggle. They need not offer us solutions, but they can battle with us in prayer.

Prayer is a vital tool for anyone to survive the wilderness seasons. Not only do we utter them to stay connected to the One Who sustains us, but we also have others utter prayers on our behalf.

Write names of people who care about you enough to pray for you. They may be imperfect people, who may not even understand this season of your life, but if they can pray for you, reach out to them. No need for explanations. Just ask them to whisper a prayer for you. Watch and see how their voices lifted to the heavens can have a powerful effect in giving you enough strength to carry on in your journey.

THE MANTLE

The firelight illuminated the dark and allowed her to see something she couldn't see while wallowing in darkness: His sustenance. So overtaken by her self-absorbed despair, she barely even realized her own hunger and thirst. Famished not only in flesh, but also in spirit.

Her grumbling stomach indicated her need, one she stopped ignoring when she realized how weak she had allowed herself to be.

Still, there it was before her, by the flame that lit up the dark night sky: a mantle of scarlet silk on the ground. On the mantle, she found a platter of meat and a glass of honeyed water.

She reached for the plate, but stopped when she remembered to close her eyes and whisper her thanksgiving to her Sustainer. She then reached for her meal as she admired the new mantle He had given her.

Her hope grew for the journey ahead. She was about to bite into her food when a hiss echoed in the silence.

Are you not His beloved? Why then did
He abandon you by the roadside to die?
So weak. So alone. Does He not care
about you?

Her mind wandered, entertaining questions and doubts justifying the slither's accusations.

<u>Did He not say He will be your strength?
If His Word is true, then why are you so
weak? Maybe He has refused to be strong
on your behalf.</u>

Even as the slither spoke, her pulse raced, but the last statement triggered a memory — one that uplifted her soul and multiplied her hope. His sweet voice had promised her He would show Himself strong to those who committed their hearts to Him.

She halted all thoughts that didn't point to His heart and mind regarding who she was in His eyes.

My heart has committed to seek the Lover of my soul, and I am in this journey to find Him.

She snickered and took a hearty bite of the meat given her. The hiss grew louder and the more it did, the more delicious her meal tasted.

She ate her fill and renewed her strength.

By the time she finished her meal, the thanksgiving of her lips drowned out the accusations of her enemy.

The sojourner began again, and with praise and thanksgiving flowing from her lips, she received from Him the strength she needed to walk on.

Manna

VERSES FOR MEDITATION

Anyone who lives on milk, being still an infant, is not acquainted with the teaching about righteousness. But solid food is for the mature, who by constant use have trained themselves to distinguish good from evil.
Hebrews 5:13-14

For the eyes of the LORD range throughout the earth to strengthen those whose hearts are fully committed to him.
2 Chronicles 16:9a

We demolish arguments and every pretension that sets itself up against the knowledge of God, and we take captive every thought to make it obedient to Christ.
2 Corinthians 10:5

AUTHOR'S REFLECTIONS

We need to grow up.

The wilderness — should we submit to His dealings while we are in it — is about preparing us for the next level. It's about depending on Him. It's about our spiritual maturity.

Infants don't belong in the wilderness. It's not a place to wallow in our unbelief or our doubt. It's not a place to act like a toddler, crying out for spiritual milk, throwing tantrums when we cannot get what we ask for.

We need to grow up and learn to distinguish between lies and Truth. We need to maintain a steady walk through the path of righteousness for His name's sake.

A lot of times, our battle with the flesh happens in our head. Our hearts are in the right place, yet our minds play tricks on us.

We reason and analyze and rationalize.

We replay and recall and rethink.

In doing so, we fall into an endless cycle, and inevitably miss out.

Sometimes, all it takes is simple faith to break out of that cycle. An honest attempt to curb our thoughts Godward. When we do so, He recognizes the choice we made for Him, and we see our circumstances in a new light. He lifts old mantles from us, and we receive new mantles of His anointing, blessing, grace, and sustenance.

When this happens, the enemy loses power over us, and once again we are able to thank Him. We are able to return to a place where praise is continually on our lips.

day 30

The Woman's Beginning

*H*er legs were strong, her heart was light, and her direction was steady. The path ahead of her was winding, long, and narrow, but her faith grew with every step, anticipating His presence at every bend of the road.

Each step she took was one step closer to her destination: the kingdom of glorious light.

How far she had already gone! The wilderness had transformed her in ways she had never expected.

He's faithful and strong! He's for me and not against me! And at the end of me, He became my beginning. My fresh start!

A fresh start. She wondered what that meant. Did it mean everything that had come before didn't count? Did her wallowing in the wayside nullify all that came before it?

Her mind was about to drift into dangerous territory, so she added a skip to her step and hummed a tune with her lips. She knew better than to allow wayward thinking to consume her.

What was behind didn't matter. Only He knew. Only He could be the judge of what among her choices and actions counted toward eternity. What mattered right now was where He was leading her. The journey brought joy to her heart. Exuberance, delight, and anticipation dwarfed any excitement she had ever felt before.

With it, however, came a deeper sense of reverence — an awareness causing her to shudder, for it showed her how great the One she loved was. Indeed, marvelous things were ahead! For He was before her, with her, and ahead of her. And whatever happened before served only to prepare her for whatever awaited her. All that happened in the past had taught her to stay low and to look up.

Light in step and glad in heart, she continued on, but soon, an eerie awareness came over her. She stopped on her tracks. Her eyes darted from side to side and assessed her surroundings. Fear absent, peace told her she was safe, but she was also not alone.

Aware of another presence — one she needed — she slowly turned around.

Sure enough, a feminine figure cloaked in white floated above the ground. The hem of her long ivory dress touched the stone path beneath. Bright light emanated from her.

"Who are you?" the woman asked.

"You may call me Lady Wisdom."

Manna

VERSES FOR MEDITATION

*God, make a fresh start in me, shape a Genesis week
from the chaos of my life.*
Psalm 51:10 (MSG)

*The fear of the LORD is the beginning of wisdom, and
knowledge of the Holy One is understanding.*
Proverbs 9:10

AUTHOR'S REFLECTIONS

Something new happens in the wilderness. It's a place of restoration and renewal, a place where we reach endings and experience beginnings. Here, a personal genesis can happen. Merriam-Webster defines genesis as a noun meaning the origin or coming into being of something. If we allow Him to have His way in us during our wilderness seasons, we can hold on to the promise of a genesis. We can expect the coming into being or the formation of something He's always planned for us.

The wilderness represents a time of preparation, a training ground for something new. After the Father established His sonship and inheritance, Jesus spent forty days in the wilderness. He fasted there before engaging in public ministry. God establishes something in us or through us during our wilderness seasons, but it is important for us to go through this time with a sense of reverence toward Him. Our journey is a holy act, meant to connect us to the heart of God.

Only when we give Him the reverence He deserves — our hearts committed to walking the path of righteousness — can He impart the wisdom we need to enter our fresh start.

We shed off the past and claim our salvation and inheritance, and we trust in His wisdom to prepare us to live out His kingdom wherever we are.

day 31

THE QUEST OF LADY WISDOM

The faceless figure of light walked forward and gestured for her to do the same. The two figures walked without a word spoken. Somehow, silence seemed wise to both the woman and the mysterious lady who had just joined her trek. Silence bred reflection and reckoning — a weaning away from what was to forge toward what will be.

Yet even as the sojourner walked, she sensed something missing. Something she needed if she was to progress in her journey, and somehow, she knew the familiar stranger would show her the way. Inquiries inundated her curious mind, but an inclined ear and a quiet heart felt like the wisest recourse. So, while waiting for Lady Wisdom to speak, she focused on steadying her breaths and shushing her mind.

"I once called out to you." Lady Wisdom spoke. "You used to ignore me, but not anymore. I imagine Folly has tried to woo you away from the path established for you. But, while the enemy has tempted you to wander many times, you've always found your way back to the narrow road. I am pleased, and I imagine He is delighted as well."

"You called out to me?" she asked.

"I called out to many. I've been everywhere, inviting anyone who would listen. Many must tread this path, but they choose not to heed His call. It's why the journey is more solitary than it ought to be. Many forsake my quest."

"Your quest?"

"The quest to find rest."

It wasn't what she expected Lady Wisdom to say. Rest seemed a strange commodity to expect in a journey through the wilderness.

"How things would change if more lived out the Father's rest! Oh, to experience the unforced rhythms of grace..."

Lady Wisdom's words and the tone by which she said it made the sojourner's heart long for an easy yoke and a light burden. The journey didn't need to be a burdensome struggle.

Lady Wisdom sounded like she knew what she was talking about, so the woman listened, for she yet had a lot to learn.

Manna

Verses for Meditation

Do you hear Lady Wisdom calling?
Can you hear Madame Insight raising her voice?
She's taken her stand at First and Main,
at the busiest intersection.
Right in the city square
where the traffic is thickest, she shouts...
Proverbs 8:1-3 (MSG)

Come to me, all you who are weary and burdened, and I will give you rest. Take my yoke upon you and learn from me, for I am gentle and humble in heart, and you will find rest for your souls. For my yoke is easy and my burden is light.
Matthew 11:28-30

Author's Reflections

The Father longs for His children. God longs for us. He posted messengers everywhere, in the highways and byways, that they may cry out: He is the Way.

Reflect on the fact that you are one of those who listened and are now in ardent pursuit of Him.

This is not a reason for pride. It does not give us a license to think of ourselves as better than others, but it is definitely a reason to celebrate, because He celebrates! Imagine His smile whenever He sees every step we take — no matter how painful, no matter how tired we are. Imagine His cheer whenever He sees us overcome. Do you sense His delight?

He celebrates! Our Father is One Who knows how to throw a grand party, a feast for those who return to Him.

He knows where we are right now, and he knows the state of our souls, as well as the condition of our hearts. He sees every God-ward decision we make.

Should we ever suffer from weary souls and burdened hearts, we must remember He longs to give us rest. The journey has its challenges, but we need not go through it weighed down by worries and anxieties never meant to be ours.

His yoke is easy, and His burden is light.

We must take time to lay them all at His feet, and while we're at it, learn to celebrate and delight with Him as well.

THE FEAST OF LADY WISDOM

"Many yearn for abundance." Lady Wisdom waved her hand in one big flourish. "But they do not see it for lack of faith."

The sojourner's eyes widened when in the path ahead of them, a house appeared, welcoming all those who passed by. "How is that possible?" she whispered beneath her breath.

"The house has been there all along, but many are too distracted to see. His Spirit has directed you toward the paths of wisdom. He has lifted the veil of confusion from you, for you have set your eyes on Him. You are one who sees. He longs for a bride with vision, not one who follows blindly. You will learn more of this when you reach the kingdom, but for now, come, I have prepared a feast for you."

They reached the house — a cottage with a lush garden in front — a place where everything had the potential to flourish.

Lady Wisdom led her inside the home and hearth of one who had insight that spanned the ages. Inside, someone had already prepared a feast, with a generous spread set over a wooden table — bread, roast lamb, and the choicest of wines.

Peace came over her as she stepped into the home.

"Come, come," Lady Wisdom beckoned. "Come sit where many sat before you. Dine with me, learn from me. The feast is a promise. This is His promise to those who seek Him out, to those who follow Him. You will lack nothing and experience abundance where it matters."

The woman took her seat, skeptical. She had left behind her possessions to pursue Him, her Priceless Pearl. She had undertaken a journey of barrenness through the wilderness. Was she now to believe He intended for her to live in abundance, after all?

"I do not speak of material possessions, child," Lady Wisdom said gently. "I speak of abundance where it matters: abundance of joy, abundance of grace, abundance of peace. What matters is the rest of our hearts, not the rest of our hands. When we possess a rested heart, we can delight in His feast, His abundance, His joy."

They said grace, and they broke bread and drank wine, and as they enjoyed the feast, clarity came over the woman.

By the time she left Lady Wisdom's Home and Hearth, she understood.

He is my Shepherd. I lack nothing.

VERSES FOR MEDITATION

Are you confused about life, don't know what's going on?
Come with me, oh come, have dinner with me!
I've prepared a wonderful spread—fresh-baked bread,
roast lamb, carefully selected wines.
Leave your impoverished confusion and live!
Walk up the street to a life with meaning.
Proverbs 9:4–6 (MSG)

The Lord is my shepherd, I lack nothing.
Psalm 23:1

You prepare a table before me
in the presence of my enemies.
You anoint my head with oil;
my cup overflows.
Psalm 23:5

AUTHOR'S REFLECTIONS

Rest and abundance, abundance and rest.

We have a Father Who wants to give us both. Our Savior made a way for us to receive. We have a Guide Who produces the fruit and the gifts stemming from the fertile soil of rest and abundance.

There is no striving here.

Wilderness journeys can sometimes feel like striving. We adapt a mentality of pushing through and never giving up. After all, we must see our journey through! How can we not strive? While this mindset can lead us to a certain point, it tends to not take into account the Father's heart — one that is after relationship. He is more concerned with the leanings of our hearts than the works of our hands.

His rest does not mean we abandon the works of our hands, for this too, He intends for good. His intent is for our work to be an act of worship toward Him, but after the curse, work became toil.

When we rest in Him, He lightens our load. He lifts the power of the curse, and we are able to delight once again. We are able to experience the fruit of our work in a way we couldn't in an atmosphere of striving.

His abundance comes with a rested, satisfied, and joyful heart — one that doesn't measure itself by accomplishment, but by our continuous relationship with a Father we can love and trust.

He wants this for us. He wants us to experience His rest and abundance. When we know this, our wilderness journeys — where we encounter His wisdom — become more of a privilege than a hard task we have to plow through.

May each of us turn the work of our hands into worship. May we learn to do it through Him, for Him, and with Him.

day 33

BELOVED

Long after she left Lady Wisdom's home and hearth, she still couldn't contain her joy over the revelation she had received. The feast gave strength to her body, the conversation nourished her mind, and the warmth comforted her heart.

She had been walking on the narrow path for what felt like ages. The road knew no end, but her heart rested in the conviction she would reach her destination as promised. Thus, daily, she took one step at a time, each step taking her closer to Him.

One morning, she expected the path to continue straight ahead like it did for the past days. Instead, after she reached the top of a small hill, the path curved toward a range of rocky mountains. She creased her brows and sped up her walk out of curiosity over what new sight would greet her. When she reached the curve to check what hid behind the range, she discovered a grove of trees in a round clearing at the foot of the mountains.

The strong flaps of countless wings echoed against the rocky mountain walls and startled her. Numerous delighted exclamations of "She's here!" reached her ears. Her mouth dropped open when a multitude of winged ones flew to her, lifted her from the ground, and carried her to the grove.

"What is happening?" she asked.

"We've heard so much about you!" a bunch of them said in unison. The pronouncement preceded a chorus of uncontrollable giggles.

Their childlike playfulness lifted her spirits and dissipated any ounce of apprehension or anxiety left in her. They set her at the center of the grove where she saw several familiar faces: the gossamer prince, the stone troubadour, and Folly. The gossamer prince's face lit up when he saw her. The stone troubadour paid her no mind as he plucked tune after tune and danced around a fire. Meanwhile, Folly perched herself on top of a large, spotted mushroom. A scowl marred her pretty face.

"His beloved is here! She has arrived!" the gossamer prince exclaimed. "Oh, the many reasons we ought to celebrate!"

The multitude of winged ones cheered. The woman then realized the grove wasn't just a grove for within it was a gate leading to a kingdom of winged ones.

The gossamer prince sat on her shoulder. "You are the beloved of the King. I am the future ruler of a kingdom allegiant to the One Whom you've given your heart to. It delights me to give you good news. Sojourner, the one I love has learned to love me as well."

The woman's face lit up in a huge smile. "You've won over Folly's heart?"

"Oh no." A hint of sadness flickered in his eyes. "Folly has chosen her path, and I've released her to follow her own whims." Delight brightened his eyes again. "I have found instead a daughter of wisdom. She is now my betrothed, my beloved."

Amidst merriment and singing, the woman smiled, for the delight of the gossamer prince over his newfound bride provided her a picture of how much the Lover of Souls delighted in His beloved: her.

Verses for Meditation

The LORD your God is with you, the Mighty Warrior who saves. He will take great delight in you; in his love he will no longer rebuke you, but will rejoice over you with singing.
Zephaniah 3:17

His pleasure is not in the strength of the horse, nor his delight in the legs of the warrior; the Lord delights in those who fear him, who put their hope in his unfailing love.
Psalm 147:10-11

There is no fear in love. But perfect love drives out fear, because fear has to do with punishment. The one who fears is not made perfect in love.
1 John 4:18

Author's Reflections

He delights in us.

The fear of the Lord leads to wisdom, and wisdom leads to His love. In His love, we find His delight.

The wilderness isn't meant to punish us or make life difficult for us. It's meant to lead us to the reality of His heart. Here, if we allow Him to, He can establish us in Him. We learn that stripped of all things, we are enough. Absent of striving and all distractions, in a place like the wilderness where we only have ourselves to offer Him, we find He wants us still. He doesn't need our striving. He doesn't need our works. It's us who gives His heart delight.

You are enough. Bring yourself to Him as you are, and let Him continue the work He has started in you. He delights in you, because He loves you.

You are His beloved. We read this in books and encounter it repeatedly in church culture. In a wilderness place, where it's you and Him and nothing else, He ingrains the knowledge of His love in us. The knowledge of His love becomes a part of who we are, erasing our fears, nullifying our striving.

We must walk out of the wilderness, fearless, because He has established us in His love.

day 34

THE GOSSAMER PRINCESS

After the celebration died down and the feasting ended, the winged ones retreated to homes hidden in the bushes, branches, and trunks of the fantastical grove. Only when everyone else had left and the woman sat alone by the firelight did the prince's betrothed reveal herself. Her countenance exuded mirth absent in Folly's demeanor. Folly projected a carefree attitude when she spoke of pursuing pleasure, but her eyes betrayed her listlessness. On the other hand, the prince's betrothed displayed an unassuming brand of abiding happiness. Her confident gait, sweet smile, and bright eyes revealed joy different from Folly's. She had rooted her pleasure and security in her intended identity.

She giggled upon seeing the woman. "I've waited so long to meet you. Forgive my delay. When you arrived, I had just rushed out to visit neighboring kingdoms to attend to several errands. Our wedding draws near, and I am swallowed up by the preparations. Oh, I'm so excited! You will come to our wedding, won't you?"

"I want to."

"Then you must! After all, you too must someday go through the preparation necessary to become a Bride. Oh, the journey you're taking! Tell me all about it! What delights have you encountered along the way?"

The sojourner gaped at the immediate sense of connection established between her and the princess, who displayed a sweet abandon with no hint of self-consciousness. "First, tell me more about you," she said. "How did this wedding come to be?"

The gossamer princess blushed. "I waited for him for so long! I thought he'd never come. When my father introduced us, my betrothed must've known immediately, because he pursued me soon after."

The woman wondered if the princess knew of the prince's love for Folly.

As if reading her mind, the princess continued, "He told me of another whom he had loved. I've heard of it from the troubadour's songs. My heart broke for him, but more for her. How blind must one be not to recognize the love offered? Unfortunately, many choose blindness over true love."

"That's because many do not recognize true love."

"With eyes, yet without sight." Momentary sadness covered the winged one's face as she placed her fingers over her eyes. "May we never lose sight of love." After she removed her hands from her eyes, her gossamer wings spread out wide. They lifted her from the ground and carried her so she could face the woman at eye level. "I'm more than acquainted with the ache of loving someone, who sometimes feels more distant than present. The One you follow is a dear friend of mine, and He has convinced me many times of this: He loves you, even when you don't feel it."

"I know," was the woman's quick response, genuine and heartfelt. "I'm not blind to His love."

The gossamer princess smiled. "For that reason alone, sojourner, you are blessed."

Manna

Verses for Meditation

For the wisdom of this world is foolishness in God's sight. As it is written: "He catches the wise in their craftiness"
1 Corinthians 3:19

I pray that out of his glorious riches he may strengthen you with power through his Spirit in your inner being so that Christ may dwell in your hearts through faith. And I pray that you, being rooted and established in love, may have power, together with all the Lord's holy people, to grasp how wide and long and high and deep is the love of Christ, and to know this love that surpasses knowledge—that you may be filled to the measure of all the fullness of God.
Ephesians 3:16-19

Author's Reflections

We live in an upside-down world. What's wrong seems right, and what's right seems wrong.

This is the way of Folly. Many people don't recognize the love of God. The idols of this world blind many by taking our time and our hearts and distracting us from a God of Love.

But this is not you. You are a Christ-follower, who is by no means perfect, but among those who have chosen Him.

The enemy will try to condemn us and accuse us every chance he gets. He's just pathetic that way. But, we have God's Spirit strengthening our inner being, and we have Christ abiding in our hearts. He has rooted us and established us in His love. His eternal, enduring love is what will carry us through the rest of our journey in the wilderness and beyond. He transforms us and makes us whole. He turns us into secure sons and daughters, because He loves us with a love so powerful, it changed the course of history at the cross.

Oh, sojourner, indeed you are loved! May God establish you in the knowledge of this every day for the rest of your life.

THE GOSSAMER WEDDING

wo kingdoms, loyal to the Most High, converged when the gossamer prince wed the gossamer princess. They and their subjects celebrated the day with a feast, music and dance, and a generous dose of laughter. Folly appeared to be the only person most unhappy amidst the merriment. Often, the sojourner noticed her with a frown on her face and arms crossed over her chest. Once, she kicked the air she floated on for no discernible reason.

Most ignored her because anyone who dared speak to her regretted the interaction. At first, the sojourner watched with mild amusement as Folly flaunted her disdain, but as the day wore on, the sojourner's heart went out to the young winged one. As she approached Folly, she felt a soft breeze caress her skin. A presence — with her all along — manifested Himself to her. Her beloved, more often sensed than seen.

"You're here," she said.

"I'm always with you."

"Does it please You to see this union between prince and princess?"

"YES. BOTH HAVE LONGED FOR THIS DAY. I, TOO, LONG FOR THE GLORIOUS DAY WHEN..." His words trailed off as Folly, with a scowl on her face, floated up and down the air past them. "DEAR YOUNG FOLLY," He said. "IT'S NOT TOO LATE FOR HER YET. I STILL HAVE HOPE SHE fiNDS HER WAY BACK TO LADY WISDOM."

"There is hope even for her?" The woman's heart leapt.

"FOR AS LONG AS THEY DRAW BREATH, THE LOST HAVE HOPE. FOLLY IS ONLY ONE AMONG THE MANY LOST. YOU WILL MEET MANY OF THEM ONCE YOU REACH MY KINGDOM AND RECEIVE YOUR MISSION."

"My mission?"

"YES. THERE'S MUCH YOU NEED TO PREPARE FOR, BUT I ASSURE YOU: I WILL EQUIP YOU FOR WHAT LIES AHEAD."

"What lies ahead?"

"THE END OF THE WILDERNESS." Before she could react, He issued a warning. "DON'T THINK YOU WILL REACH YOUR LAND OF PROMISE UNOPPOSED. THE ENEMY WILL DO EVERYTHING TO KEEP YOU FROM REACHING THE END OF THIS WILDERNESS."

"Battle awaits." In her spirit, the words rung true.

"YES, BUT REST ASSURED YOU WON'T GO UNEQUIPPED, BUT YOU MUST REMEMBER TO APPLY EVERYTHING YOU LEARNED IN THE WILDERNESS."

"Am I ready?"

"YOU WILL BE." He smiled at her. "ENJOY THE FESTIVITIES, BELOVED. LET IT REMIND YOU OF THE KINGDOM AND THE KING WAITING FOR YOU."

He disappeared and left her with a view of the gossamer prince and princess floating on the air in an enraptured dance. Mesmerized by the display of beauty and romance, she didn't notice the new addition to her wardrobe: a belt on her waist and a sword hanging from it.

Battle awaits.

Manna

VERSES FOR MEDITATION

I'm not asking that you take them out of the world
But that you guard them from the Evil One.
They are no more defined by the world
Than I am defined by the world.
Make them holy—consecrated—with the truth;
Your word is consecrating truth.
In the same way that you gave me a mission in the world,
I give them a mission in the world.
I'm consecrating myself for their sakes
So they'll be truth-consecrated in their mission.
John 17:15-19 (MSG)

"Righteous Father, though the world does not know you,
I know you, and they know that you have sent me. I have
made you known to them, and will continue to make you
known in order that the love you have for me may be in
them and that I myself may be in them."
John 17:25-26

AUTHOR'S REFLECTIONS

We are here on a mission, you and me. God meant for us not only to know Him, but also to make Him known. As we draw closer to Him, He imparts to us His heart and mind. We see ourselves in the light of His glory, but also others in the same way.

Our journey through the wilderness isn't just for our own benefit. It is also so that we will receive His mercy, His compassion, and His love for the lost. If our journey happens only to make us feel good about ourselves, then we've missed the point. He draws us to the wilderness not only to encounter Him, but also to impart upon us a vision greater than ourselves. He draws us to the wilderness to show us His glory that we might reflect it to the rest of the world.

We've all encountered someone like Folly at one point or another. We may have even judged people like her, but this is not the heart of God, nor is it the mission He has given His people.

He called us to be light upon darkness, to receive His love that it might overflow through us and into the lives of others.

The wilderness establishes our relationship with God, but it doesn't stop there. It also establishes the relationship He wants us to have with those still of the world — one that reflects His heartbeat: to seek and save the lost.transforms

day 36

THE WARRIOR'S WAY

She exchanged well wishes with the winged ones. The newlywed gossamer couple bid her farewell. She thanked them for the refreshing reprieve from her trek across the wilderness. The grove had served as a jubilant oasis, restoring her for the battles she would soon face. They sent her off with a lot of fanfare and assured her they loved her and would always welcome her in the kingdoms of the winged.

She resumed her journey, restored by the fellowship, but most of all, by the fresh encounter she had with His manifest presence. He had imparted His heart to her and gave her His joy and peace, and also His mercy, compassion, and sorrow for those still lost. Like the beautiful, enticing Folly.

She whispered a prayer for her little winged friend and the many like Folly whom she would inevitably encounter in her lifetime. Her heart raced with a newfound urgency, spurned by the knowledge that her journey would soon come to a close. His kingdom drew ever so near. She reached the top of a hill and drew a breath when she saw it manifested before her: His kingdom. On earth. Was it as it was in heaven? How she hoped it would be! She ran down the hill with full speed, but halted midway when she glimpsed an encampment standing between her and the kingdom.

She smiled.

He had warned her about this. He said it wouldn't be easy — the battle she was about to face — but He had already equipped her for it. She squared her shoulders and recalled everything He had taught her. The air crackled with pre-battle tension.

Ready, she rose up a warrior. He had already shown her the way to victory when He had caused her to understand how violent peace can be against the hordes of the enemy.

Manna

VERSES FOR MEDITATION

You will keep in perfect peace
those whose minds are steadfast,
because they trust in you.
Trust in the Lord forever,
for the Lord, the Lord himself, is the Rock eternal.
Isaiah 26:3-4

Jesus answered, "I am the way and the truth and the life.
No one comes to the Father except through me. If you
really know me, you will know my Father as well. From
now on, you do know him and have seen him."
John 14:6-7

AUTHOR'S REFLECTIONS

Keep trusting in a God, who is the Eternal Rock, solid and constant, Someone unchangeable amidst constant change.

In our journey through the wilderness, we learned to trust in Him, to trust He will come through for us. Without the peace that comes from this trust, we cannot win our battles. If we are to take hold of His kingdom, we have to win against the giants who have encamped themselves in our minds, in our hearts, in our lives. To win, we need to trust in what Jesus said and taught us in His Word. God requires a simple, childlike trust grounding us in this reality: If He said it in His Word, we believe it.

If He said He has equipped us for what's ahead, then we do not focus on our own weaknesses, on our fears, on our shortcomings. We focus on His strength, His power, His perfection. Jesus is the Way, Truth, and Life. We trust in Who He is to us, for us, and through us. In doing so, our minds become steadfast. We establish our peace, and the ones left with reason to fear and tremble are the giants. No matter how much they huff and puff, the giants realize how difficult it is to win against men and women after God's own heart.

THE BATTLE AHEAD

As she took a deep breath, she reminded herself she had nothing to fear. She held a love beyond imagination, a perfect love she could trust in. Why wouldn't she be fearless?

With His breath of life within her and His glorious strength empowering her, she gripped her sword and marched forward, each step more steadfast than the last. She drew closer to the encampment, and reality hit her. From a distance, straight across the plains from her, stood one among many giants, tall and powerful, hardened by many battles fought, many battles won.

She froze.

What am I doing?

The doubt crept in.

I don't even have an armor, nor have I ever been in actual battle.

Paralyzed in an instant, she stood rooted to her spot and hoped the giants wouldn't see her.

The voice of the enemy — already too familiar — whispered to her ear.

> You proud, insolent child. Why do you believe Him? He drew you to take a journey you can't possibly finish. Don't you see what He's done? You can't reach His kingdom. He sent you to this wilderness to die.

Recognizing the deceiver for the slithering liar it was, she shut her eyes and gritted her teeth. She fought back the doubt assailing her mind like a fiery dart. She fought to get her peace back. When she remembered His promises and the words He spoke to her, she conquered. When she reminded herself of His truth, a belt wound itself around her waist. At the sight, supernatural peace wrapped itself around her. The peace brought a steadfast mind and shoes to protect her feet. With the steadfast mind came a helmet to protect her. Belief in her salvation strengthened her heart by forming a breastplate over it. Finally, she believed in the impossible and caused faith to equip her with a shield. Fully clothed for battle, she claimed a victory she couldn't yet see.

A slithering, furious scream resounded across the wilderness's hills and plains. Where the giants gathered, the slither manifested in the frightening form of a fire-breathing dragon. She smiled. If the lying slither felt the need to intimidate her in this manner, then she surmised it feared the giants would lose to her. And so, in its attempt to threaten her, the slither encouraged her to prepare herself for the battle ahead.

Verses for Meditation

There is no fear in love. But perfect love drives out fear, because fear has to do with punishment. The one who fears is not made perfect in love.
1 John 4:18

Therefore put on the full armor of God, so that when the day of evil comes, you may be able to stand your ground, and after you have done everything, to stand. Stand firm then, with the belt of truth buckled around your waist, with the breastplate of righteousness in place, and with your feet fitted with the readiness that comes from the gospel of peace. In addition to all this, take up the shield of faith, with which you can extinguish all the flaming arrows of the evil one. Take the helmet of salvation and the sword of the Spirit, which is the word of God.
Ephesians 6:13-17

Author's Reflections

Our journey through the wilderness is about to conclude. We can smile and be full of excitement and anticipation because we're about to reach the Promised Land. But we won't get there without a fight.

The enemy is desperate at this point.

When we're close to something great, something God planned for us, we can't expect to get there without resistance, without intimidation. But we've seen the enemy do this before. We know his strategies and tactics, and by this time, we also already encountered God's power. The enemy will huff and puff and try to do everything in his strength to keep us from marching onward, but the truth remains. The God we love and serve, the God Who loves us, has orchestrated all things for the good of those who love Him.

So we smile, we laugh, and we rejoice. Though winning the battle ahead seems impossible, we know in our heart, God is on our side, so even before the battle begins, we've already won.

day 38

THE BATTLE WON

*S*he fought in the thick of battle, her sword in one hand and her shield in the other. The powerful weapons guided her instincts against the relentless attacks of her enemies. How she stood her ground was a mystery no one had time to solve. Adrenaline rushed through her as she fought with power and strength, not her own.

But the giants, who were neither of flesh nor blood, kept returning to life. They were monsters trained in battle, and they'd already seen the demise of many a warrior.

She defeated one and yet another came. And another. And another. How was the battle ever to finish when giants she had already defeated bounced right back?

She fought until she could fight no longer. Once she used up whatever strength she had left with one last blow to the enemy, she smiled at the heavens above and surrendered herself — not to her enemies, but to the Higher Power who brought her to the wilderness.

When she reached the point where she could barely keep herself standing, a loud rumble filled the wilderness. The thunder of an invincible army shook the ground she stood on. The giants fled. The dragon snarled at her. This wasn't over.

Knowing the King defeated him long ago, she smiled. "You speak truth, my Lord," she said. "You never lie." She knelt on the ground and watched her enemies flee from the King's army.

She felt a hand on her shoulder. At her Beloved's touch, her strength returned.

"You have done well." A voice familiar, yet mysterious, spoke to her.

She almost choked in tears. "What took you so long?" she asked.

"I NEVER LEFT YOU. NOT ONE MOMENT."

This, she knew to be true. Every step she had taken past the wilderness, even in her most desperate and desolate moments, she had never walked alone.

"Thank you," she said.

"ARISE, FOR YOU HAVE FOUGHT WELL AND HAVE WON THIS BATTLE. VICTORY IS YOURS."

Strength regained, she rose to her feet. Again, He was invisible and untouchable, but she sensed His presence even as she took another step past the battle fought and won. About a day's walk stood between her and her destination, and she walked on toward the kingdom awaiting her return.

Verses for Meditation

For our struggle is not against flesh and blood, but against the rulers, against the authorities, against the powers of this dark world and against the spiritual forces of evil in the heavenly realms.
Ephesians 6:12

The Lord God is my strength [my source of courage, my invincible army]; He has made my feet [steady and sure] like hinds' feet And makes me walk [forward with spiritual confidence] on my high places [of challenge and responsibility].
Habakkuk 3:19 (AMP)

Author's Reflections

We all have those giants, the ones who haunt us repeatedly. As long as we are on earth, we battle temptation. We stumble and fall. Sins we've defeated before return with a vengeance.

As we near the end of our journey through the wilderness, odds are we will fight against giants, old and new.

Fear, doubt, weakness, stress, anxiety… name it. When in transition, we are most vulnerable, but God has prepared us for this. He has warned us of the fight ahead, so with all of our strength, we fight.

But we also inevitably reach the end of our strength. In our humanness, we tire of the battle, and that's okay. He knows and understands. He is there to pull us through the battles we face in the wilderness and beyond.

And once we've gathered ourselves back together, we find out He was with us all along. He is Alpha and

Omega, and from beginning to the end, He is present. Take heart in this season of transition. Opposition and shaking will happen, but He will see us through.

day 39

THE MIRAGE

The distance between battleground and kingdom seemed endless to her. What she had estimated to be a day's walk felt immensely longer. For with every step she took forward, it's like the kingdom took two steps away from her.

The sun rose high above the wilderness, and thirst parched her throat. Sweat dripped from her brow, and exhaustion tempted her to question if she could go on any further. Yet, her heart still swelled from the victory she had just won. She still felt His presence beside her, always with her.

Little by little, bit by bit, she took a step forward. All she needed was to take it one step at a time. She remained confident in the knowledge He would sustain her, so she kept her eyes on her destination. No turning back. With her legs tired and her breathing heavy, she drew closer and closer to the kingdom, and as she did, her heart quickened with excitement.

However, when she approached the large gate serving as the main entry point to the kingdom, everything disappeared. She stopped on her tracks, unable to believe what she was witnessing. Where the grand city of light used to be, a vast wasteland appeared. The bones of the dead littered the ground. Her heart dropped, her breath caught in her throat.

All this time, had I been walking toward nothingness?

She clenched her fists. Chaos threatened to rage within her soul yet again, but she shook her head and sought the calm.

No, He told me to come here.

She fought the urge to return to where she had come from. Whether it led to a wasteland or a city of light, the path she had to take was ahead of her, not behind her. And so she walked on. One step at a time. Forward. Even if she couldn't envision the kingdom ahead. Even if logic and reason objected. She continued her journey because she believed with all her heart this was what He wanted her to do.

When she continued her trek toward the wasteland, with supernatural vision, she approached the kingdom of glory. Where dry bones scattered, an army of light arose. Where discouragement festered, she held on to faith. When she took that final step leading to the wasteland, the kingdom appeared, and along with it came a voice. His voice, laced with the sound of approval: "The kingdom is only a mirage to those who don't believe."

The sojourner, however, had already received the eyes to see.

Manna

Verses for Meditation

So we fix our eyes not on what is seen, but on what is unseen, since what is seen is temporary, but what is unseen is eternal.
2 Corinthians 4:18

It's what we trust in but don't yet see that keeps us going.
2 Corinthians 5:7 (MSG)

Now faith is the substance of things hoped for, and the sign that the things not seen are true.
Hebrews 11:1 (BBE)

Author's Reflections

Times of transition are rarely ever easy. While transitioning out of a wilderness season, we're not only met with struggle and battle, but also questioning and doubt.

We question if we're really following Him, if this is His will. It is a time when the enemy tempts us to settle. Maybe I'm really meant for the wilderness. Perhaps this wasteland is my lot.

We question our motives. Why do we desire to experience the glory of the kingdom?

We question our future. What if it's all an illusion? What if the future promised isn't worth the journey?

We question the vision and promises He has given us. What if nothing waits at the end of our journey?

In this time of transition, it's important to hold on to our faith. This is the Christian walk, and it spans not only the wilderness, but the kingdom beyond.

We set our eyes on eternity and the unseen. We cannot fully experience His kingdom until we've learned the discipline of believing Him for what we don't yet see. Once we learn it, however, the overflow of joy, peace, and possibility is endless. The kingdom is ours for the taking.

day 40

THE KINGDOM OF GLORIOUS LIGHT

*M*assive doors decked with priceless elements and studded with shimmering gemstones hindered her entry to the kingdom. She gawked at the doors, breath-taken by how beautiful they were and how small she was in comparison. What was she going to do now? She shrugged and did what was most sensible when facing a closed door. She knocked.

The doors, however, did not burst wide open. She took a deep breath and wondered what to do next. Before she could scratch her head, a winged figure appeared — larger than the gossamer prince and his bride, larger than even her. Much larger.

She stared in awe at the shining creature hovering over her.

A wide grin spread over his face. "You must be her!" he exclaimed. "Finally! We've been waiting for you. I'm Thomas."

"Hello, Thomas," she said. She waved at the giant with magnificent dragonfly wings.

"I'm guessing you want to enter the kingdom now, yes?"

She nodded.

"We can't let just anybody in. That would be rather unsafe for any kingdom, wouldn't it?"

"I pose no danger to the kingdom, I assure you."

"Oh, but you do. Men and women whose characters the fires of testing haven't yet refined can always pose a threat to kingdom living."

She gave it some thought. "Wasn't that what the wilderness was for? To refine me? To prepare me to live out His kingdom?"

"Ah! That is a good question to ask. Perhaps you are correct!" He stroked his chin with his fingers, then his brows met, and his face hardened when he saw something on her side. "You have a satchel. What's inside it?"

She lifted her satchel and showed him its contents. "I have my Beloved's letter, a gem gifted by the gossamer prince, and an eagle's feather."

His face lit up in a wide smile when he saw its contents. "Why didn't you say so? That's exactly what you need to get in! Well, aside from one other thing, that is."

She frowned. "What else do I need?"

"I'll show you." He touched her forehead with the tip of his forefinger, and it felt as if he grew larger than he already was. But then, she realized he hadn't actually grown. He had shrunk her.

"What's going on?" she asked. She cleared her throat, surprised by the change in her voice. "What did you do?"

"To enter the kingdom, beautiful sojourner, you must become as a child."

No sooner did he say the words when the doors to the kingdom swung open. She was a child with the wisdom and experience of someone who had been a sojourner in the wilderness. She skipped her way through the doors and into the kingdom. Her wilderness season was over. The glory of His kingdom awaited, and the season of the kingdom child had arrived.

His kingdom come, His will be done.

On earth as it is in heaven.

158

VERSES FOR MEDITATION

Ask and it will be given to you; seek and you will find; knock and the door will be opened to you.
Matthew 7:7

He called a little child to him, and placed the child among them. And he said: "Truly I tell you, unless you change and become like little children, you will never enter the kingdom of heaven. Therefore, whoever takes the lowly position of this child is the greatest in the kingdom of heaven.
Matthew 18:2-4

your kingdom come,
your will be done,
on earth as it is in heaven.
Matthew 6:10

AUTHOR'S REFLECTIONS

The kingdom of God is best experienced by children dependent on Him. Our wilderness seasons should establish in us the knowledge we are God's children and we can depend on Him to see us through.

When we enter His kingdom, we accept we have a lot yet to learn. We still have a lot of tests to pass, trials to go through, battles to fight. But, we've been through the wilderness, and we've trusted Him through all of it. As we enter seasons of favor and glory manifested, we mustn't forget the dependency and trust forged in our character by the fires of the wilderness.

When we humble ourselves and learn to delight in the things our Father does for His children, we live out the fullness of being citizens of His glorious kingdom.

Exciting days are ahead. It's not a time to settle, but to advance and take hold of His promises, to live out the plans, the hope, the future He has for us.

In the whirlwind of life, we must remember to return all glory and honor to the One Who breathed life in us and Whose Love sustained us in the wilderness.

May you enjoy life as a child of the king exploring everything His kingdom has to offer.

God bless you!

Author's Note

DEAR READER,

Thank you for joining me in this journey!

I started writing The Woman in the Wilderness in 2011. I wrote the story portion of Days 1-14 at a time when I was hungry for God and at a point where I wasn't certain about so many things in my life. Over five years later, it seemed like I went full circle. December of 2016, I felt like He was leading me to revisit this devotional, and so I did. Thus, I started reading the story every day, and adding the "Manna" part for the first 14 days. From Day 15 onwards, I used my prayer times and Scripture reading to write what would happen next.

And so, I completed this devotional.

If you ever got the sense I was making things up as I went, it's because I kind of was. I wrote this according to what I felt He was telling me at that particular moment. The woman's journey in this book is very much mine, and if you got this far, I'm guessing it's also yours.

I am honestly excited to see where He will lead me after this. My heart is expectant even as I believe I will experience Him and His kingdom in ways I could only imagine. That is my prayer for you as well.

I hope to hear from you in whatever way possible. Message me (find out how on my website, provided below) or leave a review on Amazon or Goodreads. It's nice to know others are on this journey with me.

God bless you! May His face always shine upon you and through you!

You are loved.

Blessings,
Joanna Alonzo
www.joannaalonzo.com

the author

A SOJOURNER

Joanna Alonzo is an author of Christian fiction novels with grit, grace, and wonder. She has a Bachelor's Degree in Information Technology from St. Louis University, but her creative leanings drew her away from software development to a career in faith and uncertainty. Her homebase is La Trinidad Valley in the Philippines, but she wanders around too much to have a permanent residence. She is a fascinated apprentice to the Greatest Storyteller of all and loves to highlight His supernatural grace in her stories. She loves having coffee chats with people, but isn't a fan of them hugging her too much. Find out more about her and her work at WWW.JOANNAALONZO.COM.

joannatheparadox

the publisher
HINENI PUBLISHING

Hineni (ינני) is a Hebrew word that means "Here am I" or "Here I am". It's how Abraham, Moses, Samuel, and Isaiah responded to the voice of the Lord when He called on them. It denotes not a presentation of ourselves as ready and totally available.

Hineni Publishing is a Philippine-based Christian company established in 2020. The heart and vision of Hineni Publishing is to produce books and literature written by "a ready scribe" seeking to please the King as in Psalm 45:1 - "My heart overflows with a pleasing theme; I address my verses to the king; my tongue is like the pen of a ready scribe." (ESV)

Find out more about it at
WWW.HINENIPUBLISHING.COM.
hinenipublishing

Printed in Great Britain
by Amazon